CONGREGATIONS IN CONFLICT

Congregations in Conflict

Tom Allen

CHRISTIAN PUBLICATIONS

CAMP HILL, PENNSYLVANIA

Christian Publications
3825 Hartzdale Drive, Camp Hill, PA 17011

The mark of ✝ *vibrant faith*

ISBN: 0-87509-448-1
LOC Catalog Card Number: 90-86215
© 1991 by Christian Publications
All rights reserved
Printed in the United States of America

91 92 93 94 95   5 4 3 2 1

Cover photo credit: Comstock

DEDICATION:

To "Pastor Bill" Goetz, my friend and mentor,
who is quick to diffuse conflict through his genuine
humility and gentle spirit. A large church in Canada
thrives today because this one man dared to believe
that "God's strength is made perfect in weakness."
Thanks for showing me and many others
the low road to greatness.

Contents

PART THREE: Resolving Church Conflict

INTRODUCTION

George Verwer, in his excellent book, *Come, Live, Die*, offers a revision of the old classic hymn, "Onward Christian Soldiers." He penned these thought-provoking lyrics:

> Backward Christian soldiers, fleeing from
> the fight,
> With the cross of Jesus nearly out of sight;
> Christ our rightful Master stands against
> the foe,
> But forward into battle, we are loathe to
> go.
>
> Like a mighty tortoise, moves the church
> of God:
> Brothers, we are treading where we've
> often trod;
> We are much divided, many bodies we,
> Having different doctrines, not much
> charity.
>
> Crowns and thrones may perish,
> kingdoms rise and wane,

But the church of Jesus hidden does
    remain;
Gates of hell should never 'gainst that
    church prevail,
We have Christ's own promise, but think
    that it will fail.

Sit here then, ye people, join our useless
    throngs:
Blend with ours your voices in a feeble
    song.
Blessings, ease, and comfort, ask from
    Christ the King,
With our modern thinking, we won't do a
    thing. (Verwer pp. 91–92)

Mr. Verwer has his finger on the pulse of problem churches throughout North America. Internal warfare has reduced many local congregations to a stagnant, status quo existence. The pastor resembles "Smokey the Bear" as he makes his weekly (weakly) rounds dousing out the fires of contention.

Some congregations become so keyed up with conflict that there is a charged atmosphere of carnal excitement over just what might happen next. Anticipation is in the air concerning just who may blow up at whom. My wife and I lived through several months of intense warfare in a church we were attending. Every time the phone rang, we were sure it was more news from the front.

The manifestation of the conflicts in the church today will appear in different ways. Some conflicts result in rival factions that refuse to speak to one another. At the other extreme, fist fights may break out from time to time. (I could name the state, city and church in the eastern United States where actual punches were thrown at a governing board meeting. There were no knock-outs, but most felt it was a good match anyway.)

Congregations develop reputations

Certain congregations develop a reputation for their rancor. They become renowned for their fierce battles, divisions and pastor-bashing. Usually a young minister, fresh out of college or seminary, is thrown into this kind of lion's den. In no time at all, this new pastor has a whole new understanding of what the district superintendent or bishop meant when he said, "I have a church that will be a real challenge for you!" Some district leaders have a strange sense of humor.

And what becomes of that young pastor thrust into the war zone at such a tender age? He will either retreat, resign or resolve. Many opt for retreating into an attitude of acceptance. "All churches have fights, and nothing can be done to stop it. I should just accept this as an occupational hazard and go about my pastoral duties." This is a safe, easy way out—at least in the short term.

A good percentage become so disillusioned that they simply resign. Some may move on to another church hoping for greener pastures, but others leave the ministry altogether. They cannot come to terms with the various contradictions implied in all the fussing and feuding. The only way out seems to be a complete renunciation of God's call on their lives. A pastor in the South said to me, "Tom, I've been through some incredible infighting in my church. For the very first time in my ministry, I am seriously contemplating a return to the secular work force." He was particularly troubled because he had enjoyed several years of successful ministry in another state.

The church is in deep trouble. As an itinerant evangelist, I noted that in a recent year, of the 33 churches in which I had preached, 25 of them were experiencing a serious level of conflict. Other evangelists and conference speakers report similar findings. Pastors and lay people agree that the ubiquity of conflict has been unprecedented in recent years.

This book examines the key reasons for congregational infighting. These are crucial to identify. The church that is in the midst of strife may not even be aware of it. A Japanese saying goes: "If you want to know about water, don't ask a fish." If we do not deeply feel that something is broken, we will not attempt to fix it. Hopefully, clear statement of the reasons for church conflict will help us see just how broken we really are.

We must also come to grips with the results of our frequent fighting. Scripture is exceedingly clear on the consequences of conflict. There are serious implications for every congregation to ponder. It is literally a life and death struggle with the destiny of eternal souls on the line. We may choose to revel in our rioting, but we cannot choose the consequences. God has selected those, and we will most certainly reap what we have sown.

Can church conflict be resolved? I believe that it can be and must be. If God has shown us the way to anything, it is the way to peace and harmony. There is hope for the most desperate divisions in the church of Christ. It is my intention to point the way on the road to resolution.

My prayer is that clergy and laity alike will be renewed through this writing. We must get on with the urgent task that is before us—the evangelization of the world that will bring back our King. Ignited by a pure passion to hear the Savior say, "Well done," let us press on toward the goal to win the prize.

Tom Allen

PART I

Reasons for Church Conflict

What are the things that today's church deems worth fighting for? It is crucial to understand the background of our battles in an effort to later describe both results and resolution. As you read the following pages, reflect on your own church experience. Some—perhaps most—of this, will sound very familiar.

The purpose of Part I is to simply identify the reasons for church conflict. Rather than stating personal opinions, it is far more important to establish the facts of churches and conflicts today. Part II will then honestly evaluate the ominous results of these conflicts, and the final section will point the way to resolution.

Worshiping in Style

Call it the *Tale of Two Churches.* Two very different congregations are meeting this Sunday in the fictitious cities of Somberville and Spiritville. Let's visit each service and see how things are going. . . .

Somberville—known as a "traditional church"—the Somberville Community Chapel opens its morning worship with a great hymn of the faith, "A Mighty Fortress is Our God." Another hymn follows and then an invocation by the pastor. Announcements are given and an offering is taken. The choir sings. The congregation stands for another hymn, and on verse four the pastor says, "The children may now be dismissed for Junior Church." After preaching his sermon, the minister calls for the closing hymn and leads in the benediction. As the organ plays the postlude, the reverend walks to the back of the sanctuary to greet the people as they exit.

All of the above is carefully, if not dutifully

recorded on the first page inside the bulletin under the heading, "Order of Worship." There are very few surprises or spontaneous events in Somberville. Week after week, the services are predictably the same. From time to time a minor innovation may be attempted, but very few changes ever actually prevail.

Spiritville—known as a "contemporary congregation"—the Grace Church of Spiritville approaches Sunday morning in an entirely different manner. In fact, it may not even be called a morning worship service—these folks may refer to it as a "fellowship gathering" or "praise gathering." The first 30 or so minutes are devoted to the singing of praise and worship choruses. Often a "worship band" or "orchestra" accompanies one or more guitarists who strum as the people stand and sing. Words are flashed onto the front wall or screen via slide or overhead projection. Some raise their hands, or clap. Many close their eyes. Others gently sway to the background music as they worship.

A pastor or elder moves to the microphone. The people are now prepared for prayer, and he leads them. Announcements may be given. The offering might be placed in a box by the exit rather than in a plate passed during the service. More choruses will be sung and perhaps special musical numbers. Though there is no written order of service, the meeting has a definite sense of direction and flow. A sermon is delivered. The closing chorus is repeated two or three times as the service concludes.

No doubt readers on each side of these contrasting worship styles have already bristled at the mere mention of "that other way." People embracing both options would like to think that their approach is more synchronized with Scripture. And those that claim to be somewhere in the middle may feel especially confident in their position. We have a real hotbed of contention here, and it does not promise to go away any time soon.

Church personalities

The dilemma seems to be this: a church, much like an individual, tends to take on certain personality and character traits with the passage of time. These special features form deep roots as the church develops its own style. Every new pastor, the generations of families who attend and the various lay leaders who come and go, all contribute to the continuation of traditions handed down through the years. When someone or some group comes along with a radical new idea for how to conduct "real worship," the traditionalist feels hot flashes of rage. The mere thought that someone would dare tamper with comfortable customs is deemed heretical.

The conflict is often non-existent in new churches that are founded on a contemporary premise. Advertising, mass mailings and phone calls of many recently planted congregations are rather up-front in their appeal to those who are tired of the "traditional" church. People who begin attending these fellowships know and appreciate ahead of time what they can expect. Such persons are attracted to the emphasis on a "new" and "contemporary" style for worship.

The real fight begins

But the real fight begins when the conservative collides with the contemporary. When I wrote this chapter, I was preaching in a church that has attempted to shift into a more contemporary style. One family expressed the inner turmoil they feel each Sunday as hymnbooks lay piled in a back room gathering dust. They are weary of repeating choruses three or four times each. They miss the depth and substance of the old hymns. They languish for the lack of any sense of variety or balance. The husband once tried to approach the pastor with his concerns about the worship style, but he was quickly rebuked by the minister's terse comment: "I like the way our worship services are going."

Today's couples and singles are challenging many long-treasured aspects of the typical church service. "We've always done it this way" no longer satisfies the inquisitive minds of 21st-century worshipers. Along with chorus singing, we see more clapping and raising of hands in what were once staid denominations. Audiences are more apt to participate in the worship with verbalized prayer requests and testimonies. The pastor's sermon inquiries are answered out loud. This is different indeed from the subdued, silent congregation that so many of us grew up in.

Threatened by change

Prayer meetings are taking on a whole new look. When I was a boy, young people often prayed with the adults on a Wednesday night. The men and boys would kneel at the altar, and the women and girls would sit in the first few pews. Various ones would pray as they felt led by the Spirit while others joined with them in oneness of heart for the request or burden. All that has changed. Young people are secluded for their own Wednesday night program and prayer time. Adults break up into small groups for more intimate supplication. I suppose Bob Dylan said it best in his song from the 60s, "The times, they are a changin'."

Many worshipers today are feeling increasingly threatened by subtle and sometimes sudden changes that are taking place. Some would refer to it as a crisis, and others speak openly about "imminent denominational splits." It cannot be neatly categorized as a "younger generation vs. older generation" struggle. Various age groups are represented with each position in the worship style debate.

The church is most definitely worshiping in style. But it is the introduction of a new style that has provoked so much strife and raised so many sincere questions. The troops are gathering! Battle plans are being drawn up! The fight is on!

CONTENTION IN THE CHOIR LOFT

Like most ministers, my father had some very interesting experiences in his first pastorate. The church had endured the same pianist since the Civil War. One Sunday, however, she failed to arrive on time for the start of the morning service. My father was aware of the fact that one of the new families in the congregation had a teenage daughter who could play the piano. Out of both innocence and desperation, he asked her to accompany the opening hymn.

About five minutes into the service, the "official church pianist" arrived in all her splendor. She could hardly believe her eyes as she glanced toward the piano. She waited for just the right moment to break in. Standing at the back of the sanctuary, the pianist stomped her foot just loud enough for everyone within a one-mile radius to hear. The startled audience turned around just in time to hear her shout: "Well just who is the pianist around here anyway?!" My father, looking for a hole to crawl into, salvaged the rest of the morning as best he could.

Someone has said that the music department of the church is the "war department." A song evangelist friend of mine likes to say, "Musicians are temperamental folks—half temper, and half mental." Others tell me that they have a friend who should sing "solo" in the choir . . . "so low" that no one can hear them! Or perhaps "tenor" . . . "10 or" 12 miles away!

We smile as we hear such stories, but contention in the choir loft is no laughing matter. So many rivalries can surface, each representing rich soil wherein conflict can grow. People so quickly forget the One for whom they are singing or playing, and they allow themselves to become embroiled in meaningless controversies.

Unholy competitions

We often see unholy competition between soloists or singing groups in the church. One soloist will resent the other one because he or she is asked to sing more often. Another singer may be angered to hear a brother or sister in the Lord using one of "his" songs. "Everyone here knows that I sing that arrangement, and that it sounds better when I do it! My voice is much more suited to that number." Groups can get caught in the trap of "dueling duets" or "quarreling quartets." They may be tempted to vie for "favorite music group" status.

"You should have been in the choir under our former director." This statement is the typical prelude to another source of contention in the choir loft. Choir members will compare the old director to the new one. One way or another, feelings are stirred for or against the current choir leader. The former director often comes out the loser because no one has had enough time to find warts on the new one!

I am familiar with a notable exception to the rule that the old director comes out the loser in the battle. This church enjoyed the ministry of the same choir director for more than 25 years. He was highly regarded and deeply respected. When he died suddenly, there was just no replacing this wonderful man of God in the minds of many. It was a long time before anyone could once again attract the choir's allegiance and admiration.

The opening story in this chapter hinted at another source of conflict in the music ministry. Some instrumentalists feel that they "own" the piano, organ, electric keyboard or whatever. As time marches on, many accompanists become strongly attached to their role in the worship service and are reluctant to share or relinquish the position. This can become an enormous dilemma for large or growing congregations where there is a steady flow of new musical talent. The problem is only compounded when the "official" organist or pianist has nowhere near the ability of that new member in the church.

An authority vacuum will inevitably produce misunderstandings and mayhem. If there is no paid staff person, choir director, or clearly designated leader, various factions will form contentious coalitions. The group is often then reduced to putting every little item up for a vote. There is little unity and no unanimity. It is a system predestined to fail and foster antagonism.

Another current debate in the realm of church music is the use of what some would call "worldly" instruments: guitars, drums, amplifiers, etc. One can actually see the pained look on people's faces when these kinds of apparatus are present on the platform. A little extra noise and rhythm can go a long way in alienating a segment of the audience. Some may even get up and walk out of the service in protest. "God will never bless this church with those drums on the platform!"

Tape and copyright debate

We are confronted today with a more stringent set of laws regarding copyrighted music than ever before. No one can deny the legitimate right of composers, writers and performers to be reimbursed for their efforts. The controversy arises when some people try to cut corners and costs by photocopying these materials. How far we go with our moral convictions is often and unfortunately tied to how far the music budget will stretch. Many choir members express ill feelings for how this issue is handled.

Once upon a time, special music was accompanied by a piano, an organ, or both. Then along came taped background music. These cassette orchestras pack a powerful punch. In their wake, we now have great numbers of unemployed pianists and organists in food lines across the country. But we also have many disgruntled worshipers who are fed up with the use of this technology, and yearn for a return to live accompaniment. For some, the feeling is based on the multitude of tape malfunctions that one must endure in a given year of special numbers. Others struggle with the very act of using "canned music." These folks are hardpressed to put their concern into words, but something about it just doesn't seem right.

Contention in the choir loft can also result from the use of musicians who are not really gifted in the musical realm. Without a doubt, many who sing or play instruments in our churches have a good heart and pure motives. Unfortunately, this is not a guarantee of quality, nor is it an indicator of spiritual giftedness. As one wrong note is played or sung right after another, some saints squirm while other saints squawk.

"Why can't we have any quality control around here?"

"Now wait a minute, brother—his heart is in the right place."

"Yeah, but why can't his *voice* be in the right place, too?"

We should also face another fact of church life today: not everyone who wants to have a public music ministry has a good heart and pure motives. Some are doubtless driven by carnal desires to be seen and heard. Their concern is not primarily the glory of God and the edification of the body of Christ. Promoting self and stroking the old ego are their real interests. The use of this kind of individual becomes an understandable source of dissension. It is sad but true that many smaller groups feel obligated to use these self-promoters for the sheer lack of any other option.

In the chapter on worship styles, I hinted at another critical element of the musical war zone—contemporary vs. conservative music. Choirs are divided over this issue. Soloists and singing groups grapple with the varied tastes of the audience before them on Sunday. Believers are debating the relative merits of this or that style of music and its overall effect on worship, church life, and church growth. The pros and cons are not always black and white, and many of the battles seem to be fought on gray turf.

"Speak to one another with psalms, hymns and spiritual songs. Sing and make music in your heart to the Lord, always giving thanks to God the Father for everything, in the name of our Lord Jesus Christ" (Ephesians 5:19–20). Paul makes it sound so simple, so lovely, so pleasant. Perhaps it is. Maybe it can be.

Persecution in the Pulpit

A Canadian pastor, whom I'll call "Jim," phoned one day and talked with me for more than an hour. He was struggling with the painful experience suffered in his most recent church.

It started when he was candidating in what would be his third church. It was a small congregation of 75 people, but they had a lovely church building and parsonage that were both debt-free. During the interview, the governing board said to Jim, "We will not be able to pay you what we paid the former pastor—at least for now. But we promise that by year's end, your salary will be at that level." Jim and his wife, encouraged by this remark, decided to accept the call to pastor the church. They began their ministry in August.

It didn't take long at all for two influential couples in the church to figure out that the board had guaranteed the new pastor a rather large raise following his first five months of ministry. They even worked out the "percent-age increase"—65 percent. Even though the minister had started with the bare minimum, these two rabble-rousing families began imme-diately to criticize the decision of the board. They were equally appalled by the willingness of Jim and his wife to accept such a rapid raise in pay. One of the men said to Pastor Jim, "If you were a real man of God, you would refuse this raise!"

The level of gossip increased and intensified. While the pastor was away for his district con-ference, a committee was formed to "keep an eye" on the minister. A new family started to attend the church, and they had a profound reputation for pastor-bashing—in three pre-vious churches, this couple had engineered the dismissal of each pastor. And you guessed it—the two families who were so steamed up about the 65 percent raise just happened to get together with the new troublemakers. These three couples were able to arrange a congrega-tional meeting while the pastor was out of town. A list of accusations was drawn up, read to the church, and a vote of confidence was taken. It wasn't even close. Confidence in the new minister plummeted far below the 50 per-cent level.

Pastor Jim and his wife returned to discover that their ministry was coming to an abrupt end. Even though the congregational meeting was illegal according to church by-laws, Jim was left with no real choice but to resign. When the pastor was finally able to share his side of the story and answer each accusation, the church was traumatized and split. Forty-five people left the church and 30 decided to stay.

This minister is now an insurance salesman/investment counselor. During the dark hours of his post-pastoral depression, not even one minister in his district called to console or comfort him. Jim and his wife were left alone to sort out the confusion of this enormous conflict.

Pastors under attack

We could all wish that the story of Jim and his wife were an aberration. But in church after church, I meet pastors who feel under attack by both Satan and the saints.

In the March 26, 1990 issue of *USA Today*, an article entitled, "Vocal Congregations Make Clergy Jobs Less Secure" revealed these shocking statistics. The Southern Baptist Convention reported a 31 percent increase in clergy firings since 1984. During an 18-month period ending in 1989, 2,100 ministers were fired.

I am aware of the fact that ministers have made, are making, and will make mistakes. I don't endorse the past when the preacher was on a pedestal, exalted high and above the sin and temptation of the laity. We have all seen the utter nonsense of that old world view and I hope we have slammed the door forever on that notion. But much of the persecution in the pulpit today is pitiful, petty, senseless and silly.

Pastoral style

Some congregations want a "task-oriented pastor" while others earnestly desire a "people-oriented pastor." Given God's sense of humor, He usually arranges for just the opposite to occur. Lay people are constantly saying to me, "Well, our pastor is wonderful with people, but he's not much of a preacher." Or, "Our minister is one of the best preachers you will ever hear, but he's not much for visitation." Our churches seem to be convinced that out there somewhere is a man who can preach like Whitfield, spend hours on the porches of parishioners, and still find time to mow and trim the church lawn.

I know of this struggle firsthand because of inevitable comparisons to my father. My dad is an incredible "people person." He only requires privacy in a bathroom. Bill Allen has always taken people along on trips, and he would rather be out in the neighborhoods than behind closed doors at the church office. He viewed sermon preparation and administrative duties as necessary evils of the ministry— something that just had to be done in between numerous contacts with people.

Rev. Tom Allen, however, has taken a different approach altogether. My first love is sermon preparation and delivery. My ministry has not been marked by extensive social relationships. It took me awhile to come to grips with the fact that my father and I were different in this aspect even though we were very much alike in other areas.

And this is precisely the point. People are different. Pastors are different. God prepares each one uniquely and then dispatches them to the place where they can have a maximum impact. There are times when, in our humanity, we may botch up the pastoral selection process. In general, however, we can be confident that our Lord Jesus is 100 percent accurate in His pastoral placement skills. He has a plan and a place. And He makes no mistakes.

Democratic or autocratic?

Another way in which ministers can be very different is represented by the two words, "democratic" and "autocratic." Some lay persons have said to me, "Our pastor is just not a pacesetter—we need some strong leadership around here!" Others have made this comment: "I wish our minister were more open-minded—he can be so dogmatic and decisive." Once again, we see that conflict can arise over personality characterizations. Some pastors are very autocratic in their approach, and the churches they are serving are in need of that kind of guidance right now. The minister across town may be very democratic in his style. He always seeks the opinions of his leaders and laity. It is not that either way is *the right way*; rather, it is a matter of two different men operating in the way that God has led them with the best interests of the church in mind.

Are wives staff members?

There is also much persecution in the pulpit concerning the preacher's wife. Some churches expect her to be the "Super Wife" who meets each need of her family, works part time and chairs every committee that has anything at all to do with women. And a few ministers' wives could be content with that scenario and do a good job in each facet. But more often we see a tug-of-war develop. The women of the church are anxious for the pastor's wife to lend legitimacy to their programs and projects, and the wife is struggling to balance other family and financial needs. The minister himself is often caught in the middle, trying to appease both sides.

I have heard ministers' wives say, "They may have hired my husband to be the pastor of this church, but they didn't 'hire' me along with him!" Though we can question the spirit with which this statement is made, we cannot question its accuracy. In the truest sense of the word, she was not employed by the church, and there is no binding "job description" for the wife of a minister. (Though no doubt many would be willing to provide one upon request!) These are things that must be carefully, thoughtfully discussed. The arrangement will no doubt turn out a little differently with each spouse. Unfortunately, these issues tend to be discussed in pious little prayer groups behind the back of the preacher's wife. It only takes a spark to get a fire going.

The pastor's family is often a target of persecution and friction. People begin to pick apart the parenting style of the minister and his wife. If someone catches them having harsh words or a disagreement, the word rapidly spreads to the congregation. The "PKs"—preacher's kids—are supposed to be a cut above the "OKs"—ordinary kids. Having been a PK myself, I can testify that we do indeed feel the pressure to be a model for other children to follow. Rarely does the pastor's family measure up to the great expectations of the church. People soon discover that the minister and his wife can actually have strong disputes. Their children may go through periods of rebellion just like other teenagers. Why, that preacher's family might even miss devotions once in awhile!

Pastor's salary

As indicated in the opening story of this chapter, the pastor's salary and benefits can become a notable hotbed of contention. There would appear to be two schools of thought among lay persons on this issue: the pauper pastor and the professional pastor. Those who opt for the "pauper pastor" feel that a minister should just accept the fact that he is following in the footsteps of Jesus, and he should therefore not expect to own a home, a good car, or have nice clothes. Others see their minister as the "professional pastor." He should behave like and be compensated as a professional in the workplace. Such folks would want the minister to live comfortably in the mid-range of the local setting for salary, housing and benefits.

Opposing opinions

Problems arise when the paupers and the professionals find themselves on the same governing board or salary review committee. One side fears that a well-compensated preacher may not be able to relate to the blue collar worker or the unemployed, and he will miss valuable lessons of living by faith. The other side argues the importance of being fair and paying the pastor according to his professional status in the community. And the minister himself most often must sit back in silence as the debate goes on around him.

I spoke with a minister of music who was confronted by an elder in his church. This pastor's salary as an assistant was meager, and periodically the church would allow him to travel to other churches as a song evangelist for their crusades. He received an honorarium for these outside meetings, and it helped make ends meet for his family. But the elder was incensed at the thought of this extra income and said to him, "How can you accept those honorariums in good conscience when we are paying your salary?" When the pastor offered to compare salaries, the church leader walked away in disgust.

He's not a Swindoll

But perhaps the most widespread form of persecution in the pulpit today centers around the pastor's preaching ministry. I could not count the number of churches where someone has whispered in my ear, "We could sure use a pastor who really knows how to preach the Word!" Some have even embarrassed me by adding, "Someone like you, Rev. Allen." I am more frustrated than flattered by such statements because I know in my heart that those same people would grow tired of Tom Allen, too.

I have a theory for why so much criticism is being hurled at pulpit ministries today. I refer to it as "Great Expectations." After seeing a Chuck Swindoll video on Friday, and hearing John MacArthur on the radio on Saturday, the parishioner often goes to church on Sunday with the attitude, "Well, preacher, let's see if you can top that!" And of course, he cannot "top that." He was not surrounded by dozens of staff during the week who could take care of a thousand and one other duties and details. He was not able to enjoy the same quality time for concentrating on sermon preparation. So, devout little prayer groups form and rumors begin to circulate. "Pray that our pastor will begin to preach the Word more effectively."

This is not to imply that a congregation should not pray for the pastor's pulpit ministry. Nor can we pardon the minister who is not doing his very best to prepare sermons each week. But we need to face the fact that because of cassettes, videos, radio and TV, our "great expectations" have been exaggerated all out of proportion. The average church member wants a pastor who can preach like their hero on TV or radio and who will stay in his church of 150 people for 30 years while never expecting a raise!

I could only chuckle at the statement of a board member in the South where I was crusading. He said, "As soon as we can get rid of this pastor, we plan to get one who can preach like . . . " and he named his favorite TV minister. I just didn't have the heart to tell him that a person with preaching gifts like that would not even return a letter from his congregation of 200 people. But he found out in due time.

The *USA Today* article referred to earlier (March 26, 1990) stated: "Experts say congregations expect pastors to have the polish of television preachers and deliver membership growth like corporate sales executives."

There are problem pastors. Some ministers

have a desperate need for church discipline. Grievous words have been spoken and evil deeds have been done by men of the cloth. Preachers are sometimes guilty of building a power base for self instead of the Savior. But the church today, in the midst of its pastoral firings and hirings, needs to seriously consider the charges being made. Can the accusations be verified and justified? Is the persecution in the pulpit a proper venue or a personal vendetta? Answers to these questions are vital indeed. The pastor's spiritual reputation and ministerial future is on the line. And be assured that God will monitor our deliberations closely.

CHAPTER

4

A Woman's Place

Shortly after I arrived at a church in the
eastern United States, the pastor took me
on a tour of the building. This is not usually a
thrilling, life-changing experience for me, because when you've seen one Sunday school
wing, you've seen them all.

When we got to the sanctuary, I noticed that
there was a podium on the floor level, just
below the pulpit on the platform.

"Is this where you make your announcements?" I inquired innocently.

"No. We just finished our missions con-
ference, and one of the missionaries was a
woman," he answered. "We don't feel that a
woman should address the congregation from
the platform level, so when she spoke, she
stood here at this podium on the floor."

After nearly fainting in response to this comment, I regained my composure and had a
rather lively discussion with the pastor about
women in ministry. He was a bit distressed be-

cause I was not impressed with the "strong, scriptural stand" he and his board had taken in this regard. And this story serves to illustrate the kind of attitude that can generate gossip, bitterness and warfare in the body of Christ.

Regardless of how you and I may feel about the role of women in the church or "women in ministry," we can all agree on one thing: this can become a real hornet's nest of contention. Some churches now have their first woman on the governing board, and certain charter members have lost a few nights sleep over it. "Before long, the women will take over this church!" they say.

Radical reformation

A woman's place in society is undergoing a radical reformation. John Naisbitt and Patricia Aberdene, in *Megatrends 2000*, relate some startling statistics.

Since 1972 the percentage of women physicians has doubled. The percentages of women lawyers and architects have nearly quintupled. . . . Women hold some 39.3 percent of the 14.2 million executive, administrative, and management jobs . . . nearly double the 1972 figure. . . . Women make up 49.6 percent of accountants, compared with 21.7 percent in 1972. . . . At Apple Computer, 30 percent of the managers are women, as are 40 percent of the professionals. (pp. 224–225)

More and more young women are training in Christian colleges and seminaries for specific career ministries in youth, Christian education, counseling and other staff positions. Though evangelical, fundamental churches have not approved the ordination of women as in some mainline denominations, clearly the roles and rules are changing. There is a justifiable uneasiness among us as we enter into this issue and all of its implications.

What does Scripture say?

There are some perplexing references in Scripture. It is clear that God has always used women as His servants. Some of them have enjoyed the Lord's blessing in positions of authority, leadership and prominence on a national level. (See Judges 4:4, Second Kings 22:14, Luke 2:36, Acts 21:9 and Romans 16:1–3.)

It is also apparent that the Bible does not support a woman exercising authority as an elder in the church. "I do not permit a woman to teach or to have authority over a man," Paul says in First Timothy 2:12. Numerous references are made to the assumption that the "elders" will be men. (See First Timothy 3:2, Second Timothy 2:2 and Titus 1:6.)

One pastor summarized his findings on the issue of women in ministry with this statement:

"Women may properly engage in any kind of ministry according to their spiritual gifts just as men do, except that which involves elder authority."

The General Assembly of The Christian and Missionary Alliance in Canada adopted the following declaration during its 1988 gathering after a six-year study on the role of women as elders:

> It is recognized that the historical and biblical pattern has been that elders in the church have been men. The weight of evidence would imply that this pattern should be continued.

Both of these statements are commendable and well-stated, but they do not address themselves to the finer points. There are still many items for disagreement and dissention, and our churches appear to have found each little one. Questions still arise over the contradiction implied by the larger ministerial role that women can have overseas compared to what is acceptable in North America. Some wonder if a woman can teach or preach in a mixed audience, or if they should be limited to speaking only to other women. Others argue for or against the appointment of women to governing boards, leadership councils and key committees of the church.

Most of us do not struggle with the basic

prohibition implied throughout God's Word concerning women as elders. Confusion and conflict arise from the ramifications of that initial pronouncement. Like politicians debating the wording of laws, we can agree on the bold print, but we get tripped up on the fine print of the paragraphs below.

Tragically, in the midst of this debate, some congregations have suppressed the spiritual gifts of their women. There is a growing frustration and resentment among women who feel that they are limited to serving in nurseries or serving up noodles at a potluck supper. Many of these women do an excellent job in disguising their irritation, but sooner or later, the teapot will have to whistle. Let's hope someone is listening with an open mind and a loving heart when it does.

The Battle
of the Budget

Alayman asked me out for lunch one day to discuss a conflict with his pastor. One of the appliances in the parsonage needed to be replaced. This man had been appointed by the church board to assist the minister in finding a new one. The layman and the pastor agreed on a ballpark figure, and the pastor proceeded to purchase the applicance. That's when the trouble began.

When the bill came in, the layman thought that the "ballpark" had grown considerably since he had talked with the minister. The pastor bought one of the better models for the sake of his wife who did more than her share of entertaining in the home.

"I think our pastor is materialistic in this area—he always seems to want the best of everything," the layman said to me.

"But wouldn't you want your wife to have

the better appliances if one needed to be replaced in your house?" I responded.

"Well, probably . . . but he's the pastor! I didn't think a real man of God would have to have the top-of-the-line."

This layman had even contemplated leaving the church over this little spat. He was not willing to sit down with the pastor and discuss his dissenting attitude. The minister was struggling with materialism, and that was that.

A hotly contested issue

The fury over finances. The debate over dollars. The battle of the budget. This has become one of the most hotly contested issues in today's church. Money matters are no longer considered minor or mundane. Contemporary Christians are quick to question. A sarcastic tone can be detected in the voices of the saints when it comes to financial concerns in the congregation.

One reason for this is easy to spot: the catastrophe at PTL has left a bad taste in the mouths of many lay people. They no longer feel that their spiritual leaders can be "automatically" trusted. Thousands were taken to the cleaners by a smiling Jim Bakker, and present day believers intend to see to it that this does not happen again. A fragile confidence was broken that will not heal overnight. Ministers have been put on notice, and the congregation is looking closely at all aspects of church finances.

Treasurers may not even be credible. Just recently I heard the story of a church treasurer who was caught skimming the offerings. He looked at it as a "temporary loan" until he could manage his debts, but it became an obsession. It wasn't long until the money he owed the church was more than all of his debts combined.

The church-going population is demanding more strict guidelines for accountability than ever before, and this new emphasis should be welcomed by all. But there is a downside. With more and more people looking into the financial records of the congregation, greater numbers want a say in why, how and where money will be spent. The position of local church treasurer these days is not usually an enjoyable one.

Feuds over spending

As the opening story of this chapter illustrates, many feuds erupt over parsonage-related matters. Pastors often resent having to contend with a house that is less than ideal. There is the carpet that was both popular and installed during the Kennedy administration. Walls are painted and wallpapered in "interesting" tones and styles. Appliances are frequently on the fritz in a home that is to be the center for many dinner parties and social gatherings.

When cash is needed to remedy some of these dilemmas, a debate is triggered as to just what kind of lifestyle a pastor should exemplify in the local community. Lay people grapple with the extremes, and try to locate the middle somewhere between poor and plush. Conflicts ensue in the process of trying to find that happy medium.

Special offerings

Differences of opinion also prevail in the arena of special offerings and crisis needs in a congregation. Churches today are inundated with special requests from parachurch organizations. Everyone wants to make their presentation, and many of these represent legitimate, necessary ministries. But where does one draw the line? How many special offerings are too many? This is another area that is subject to political maneuvering. If a leader or large giver in the church presents one of his pet projects, it will most likely be received with warmth and enthusiasm. Other "less important" members in the congregation may not even get their causes placed on the agenda of a board meeting.

This controversy over giving to outside ministries becomes particularly intense for those who are committed to "storehouse tithing." Based on the principle in Malachi 3:10, some Christians feel very strongly that the tithes of God's people should remain "in the storehouse"—that is, the church. What a person does with anything above the tithe is a personal matter, but most believers today would barely qualify as tithers—those who give a minimum of 10 percent of their incomes.

Crisis needs

How does one define a "crisis need"? Too many people have heard one too many "boy cry 'wolf.' " I heard of one young girl who was used to getting an annual grant from the church so she could attend summer camp. Supposedly, her parents were poor and she would have had no other way to get to camp. One evening, her father showed up at a social gathering with his new $1,300 video camera. By some strange miracle, he was able to come up with the $75 for his daughter to go to camp that next summer.

This is a very difficult aspect of the ministry nowadays. It is not easy to differentiate between legitimate needs and irresponsible behavior. In the course of a given year, dozens of poor or homeless people pass through the church looking for a handout of food, shelter or money. Some congregations have been burned by professional con artists and now find it difficult to empathize with those who may really need help.

The debt-free debate

Then we have the "debt-free debate." Some

strong voices are being raised these days on behalf of doing everything related to the church without incurring debt of any kind. This person says, "Let's trust God to raise the cash that is needed before we build that new sanctuary!" However, there is another side to the coin of faith. Others would define faith in terms of trusting the Lord to enable His people to make payments on a conventional loan. Good, godly people can espouse opposite views on this issue. Getting them to understand and cooperate with each other can be a herculean task.

The battle of the budget is often waged during a new building program. Struggles abound concerning the structural design, the prioritization of square feet for sanctuary, Sunday school and office space, lobby dimensions and a host of other related items. Disagreements must be resolved concerning the choice of carpets, curtains, colors and pews. And look out if the building committee fails to consult a builder who attends that fellowship! (Just for the record, as of this date no one has built a church that satisfied 100% of the congregation.)

The Word of God is replete with warnings and exhortations about money. We are told to cheerfully give it (2 Corinthians 9:7). We are encouraged to store up "treasures in heaven" instead of "treasures on earth" (Matthew 6:19–21). We are cautioned that the love of money is a root of all kinds of evil (2 Timothy 6:10). We are admonished not to show favoritism to the wealthy among us because God is not impressed with rich people and they may exploit us (James 2:1–7). Money cannot satisfy the deeper spiritual needs of the human heart (Ecclesiastes 5:10). Riches will lead many into eternal perdition (Mark 10:17–23).

Fallen human nature dictated the need for so many references to money throughout the Bible. It should come as no surprise that so many conflicts in the congregation are rooted in financial matters. Apart from the grace of God, all of us are primed to attack each other, demand our rights and stand our ground. Apparently, many Christians today have opted to act apart from the grace of God.

Doctrinal Debates

We referred to them as "The Great Roommate Debates." These were the intense, extremely deep discussions of immense doctrinal issues during the formative years of Bible 101 in a Christian college. Most of us seemed to peak in our theological prowess sometime during the sophomore year. It has been downhill ever since.

I am a graduate of Asbury College, and I was raised in a Wesleyan-Arminean tradition. I had a roommate that grew up in the Plymouth Brethren Church. As you might have guessed, we were known to have lengthy deliberations on the issue of eternal security.

"Jesus said that no man shall pluck them out of my hand," Bill would say.

"Yes, that's true," I would reply. "But who says a person could not jump out of His hand if he chooses to?"

"Well, Paul said that nothing can separate us from the love of God!"

"Yes, but a person can separate himself from that love by willful, persistent sinning!"

This would go on for hours. I was always wanting to turn to Hebrews while he was ever anxious to get into Ephesians. No one ever "won" those debates, but we had a lot of fun trying. As I look back, it seems that I had more answers then than I do now.

Many churches today have been devastated by doctrinal debates. Rather than a friendly give-and-take, some Christians take their positions so seriously that relationships with people are jeopardized. Congregations are divided, families are torn apart and pastors are being fired because of theological quarrels.

The central truths

Someone has described the doctrinal spectrum in terms of a target used by an archer. In the middle of the target is the "bull's-eye." This represents the central truths of evangelical Christianity—those teachings that must be endorsed for a person to be truly born again. Dogmas such as the divine inspiration of Scripture, the virgin birth of Christ, our Lord's deity, salvation through the atoning death of Jesus, His literal death and bodily resurrection, the return of Christ, the reality of heaven and hell—these doctrines would constitute the "bull's-eye." There is no room for compromise here.

The second aspect of doctrinal matters might

be called "collective conscience." Regardless of denomination, Christians generally agree on the importance of daily devotions and faithfulness to the services of the church; abstaining from drugs; caring for the lost locally, nationally and internationally; obeying the laws of the land.

Division that causes splits

The third circle of the target could be called "individual scruples." This is the area where there is division among believers. That division has caused church splits and the formation of new denominations. This would include such weighty matters as the length of Jesus' hair, the authorship of Hebrews, why Christ wept at the tomb of Lazarus, the pronunciation of "Habakkuk," mode of baptism, eternal security, prophetic interpretation and a host of other minor league matters.

Some Scripture verses are more consequential than others. Every part of the human body is important in the interests of the whole, complete body. But the little finger is not as vital as the heart or liver. That finger can be severed without threatening a life, but remove the heart or liver and a person will die immediately! So it is with God's Word—every verse in the Bible is important in the interests of a complete Scripture, but some are more critical than others when taken individually.

We should commend or even applaud the

church that splits over "bull's-eye" matters. But our conflicts today seem to be focused on the issues of "individual scruples." Many have widened the battle zone to include doctrinal items that godly and intelligent scholars have disagreed over for centuries. And some are fighting in these gray areas as if their very salvation depended on it.

There are pre, mid and post-tribulationists. One group feels certain that the church will be raptured prior to the tribulation. Others claim with conviction that Christ will come for His church during the middle of the seven-year period, just before the three-and-a-half years of "The Great Tribulation." A third school is equally adamant about the parousia occurring "after the tribulation of those days."

"That guy is so pre-tribulation in his eschatology that he won't even eat Post Toasties!" We should be able to enjoy that little touch of humor, but for some folks, "Them's fightin' words!" The joy and expectation of Christ's coming has been diluted in our churches by manifold arguments. We are more concerned with the finer points of Revelation than we are the factual promise of His return.

Bible versions

"If the King James Version was good enough for Paul, then it's good enough for me!" I can only hope that this statement was never actually made. But I am fearful that similar words have actually been spoken in the turmoil over translations. I once had to stand and listen to a man's 45-minute lecture on the evils of using any other version but the King James. The pastor could have rescued me, but he was having too much fun watching me dangle on the end of the rope. Even worse than that, the lecturer had breath that could have slain a dragon.

The issue of Bible translations is a hot button for many believers. Fierce fighting erupts when the pastor or any other speaker even alludes to a version other than their own. These people are determined to make everyone else toe the line to their preference. Anyone who disagrees just doesn't understand how God speaks to this generation. In the past few years, some brave souls in my denomination have decided to change Bible quizzing from the KJV to the NIV. It is truly amazing that recent International Bible Quiz Championships have not been boycotted or bombed.

Eternal security and other issues

The "eternal security" debate has sent many boxers into the ring of congregational conflict. One can almost hear the ring announcer and the bell signaling "Round One." Punches are thrown from this passage and that as the opponents seek to inflict the knock-out verse into their victim. These bouts are often bloody, and we can only wonder how people supposedly filled with the love of Christ can be so violent and vicious.

Another doctrinal dispute centers around the mode of baptism. We are told that one reason for the great variety of Baptists today goes back to old arguments concerning methods of baptism.

To those who sprinkle water, the immersionists say, with tongue in cheek, "When someone dies, you don't sprinkle dirt on them—you bury them!" Debates arise over bending the candidate backwards, forwards or just letting them sink straight down.

Can physical healing be found in the atonement of Christ, or is it unrealistic to expect miracle cures in today's world? Good people can be found on both sides of this issue. The whole question of the gifts of the Holy Spirit and their role in the contemporary church is center stage and impossible to ignore. (See the chapter entitled *Charismaniacs and Charisphobics*.)

A very necessary and natural question arises. Why has God constructed His Word in such a way that there is so much latitude on the peripheral issues? Would it not have been much easier for all of us if He had simply made every issue "black and white"? There appears to be room for argument and we don't like it one bit. As human beings, we are on a quest for absolute truth, but Scripture sometimes seems to raise questions rather than answer them. Just what is God up to, anyway?

Points to realize

First, we should recognize that we "see through a glass darkly" (1 Corinthians 13:12, KJV). That is, our spiritual insights are limited in these bodies with these brains on this planet. We do not yet "know as we are known." We will someday, but not now. The omniscient God has chosen to hide some things from us for a little while. He has His reasons for this, and they are all good ones.

Second, we can rest in the assurance that our Lord has revealed all of the absolute truths we need to know in order to function in this life and the world to come. Nothing has been withheld that would keep us from safely arriving at our heavenly home. The "bull's-eye absolutes" of God's Word are sufficient for our daily needs here and hereafter.

Third, it is comforting to know that no individual theologian or minister can claim a corner on the truth. The outer rings of doctrinal debate will always be open to diverse opinions. The Bible is written in such a way that man is humbled by divine mysteries. The half has never been told, and the depths have never been fully plumbed. We all have more to learn.

Fourth, God no doubt wants to teach all of us how to "agree to disagree agreeably." It is no mere coincidence that Paul placed the premier importance of "love" in the middle of two chapters that addressed a leading theological debate of his day. The point was that every discussion, doctrinal or otherwise, deserves the context of genuine love and caring. One of the incredible ironies of our day is to hear angry debates concerning the gifts of the Spirit among those who display little, if any, of the fruit of the Spirit.

The church is overrun with scriptural sheriffs armed with their doctrinal derringers and holiness handguns. Some have learned the fine art of blowing away their adversaries with the sheer force of their arguments. When the dust settles, a church may be split, a friendship splintered or a pastor sent packing. But at least they made their point. To them, that's all that matters.

When Christians Fail

In many ways, they were a typical young Christian couple engaged to be married. They faithfully attended church with their families, and the congregation was looking forward to their wedding. The young man and his bride-to-be had selected the apartment where they would live after the honeymoon. Happy days were just around the corner.

But suddenly, everything changed. A few weeks before the nuptials, in an unguarded moment, the couple engaged in sexual intercourse. They asked God to forgive them. However, their guilt would not subside, and they confessed their sin to the pastor. He acknowledged their repentance and indicated that he would let them know what the next step would be.

A few days later, the pastor called them both to his office. "I think that you should make a public confession of your sin before the church next Sunday morning. It would be unfair for the audience at your wedding to think of you both as virgins. I will arrange for a time for you to tell the congregation," he said.

The young couple felt that this kind of restitution was a bit harsh, but they went through with it to please the pastor. Their confession sent shockwaves throughout the congregation. The people were not stunned with the couple's admission of sin as much as they were startled by the pastor's insistence on a public announcement. It was an unjustified, inappropriate request that led to an unnecessary invasion of privacy.

The incident caused no little uproar. The parents of the bride and groom were humiliated by the public disclosure of their children's sexual indiscretion. The church was divided between those who felt the pastor did the right thing and those who thought his handling of the matter was despicable. The wedding ceremony proceeded as scheduled because "the show must go on." But it was a sad and unpleasant day.

Unbiblical church discipline

Our *reaction* to the sins of Christian brothers and sisters can sometimes lead to blunders that are worse than the original failure. Church discipline, when administered improperly, will often be more damaging than any act of indiscretion. The pastor's demand for a public confession from this young couple was totally unnecessary and the body of Christ suffered more because of this needless revelation.

Unbalanced, unbiblical discipline has fueled many congregations in conflict today. The need for correction among the saints is indisputable. I have given an entire chapter to this vital subject later in the book. However, this must be carefully executed with Christlike love, understanding and forgiveness. Otherwise, the church becomes just another corporation with employers chastising employees.

Harm can so easily be inflicted on the body of Christ in the name of "scriptural church discipline." Some church leaders almost seem discouraged if there is no one around who needs to be confronted with sin. Like the Maytag repairman, they are disheartened for the lack of broken appliances. This kind of restlessness can lead to creating a crisis that did not exist.

Looking the other way

Some churches declare war because the pastor and the leadership have looked the other way in the face of obvious iniquity. Instead of dealing with the matter head-on in compassion and boldness, the spiritual leaders ignore the problem. When respected, powerful families in the congregation are involved, the temptation is often greater to overlook any wrongdoing.

We have a tendency to think of sin only in terms of "committing" certain acts. But evil can also be accomplished when we are guilty of "omitting" items. Churches today are boiling with contention because of the "sins of omission"—things that are not being done that ought to be done when Christians have failed.

In one church, a 13-year-old boy was accused of molesting a three-year-old girl. Many complained that the pastor and the elders never tried to arrange a meeting between both sets of parents even though one side expressed a willingness to convene and resolve the issue. Eventually the little girl's parents felt they had to leave that congregation. A sin of omission had left them with no alternative.

As illustrated earlier, the way in which sin is confessed is as important as the admission itself. Private issues—those matters of the mind that have not been put into action—should be disclosed to God alone. Personal sins—those wrong actions between individuals—must be acknowledged on a personal level between the parties involved. And public offenses—the evils which affect a group of people—ought to be confessed before the offended assembly. The point of the Matthew 18:15–20 passage is that we should try to keep the circle of confession as small as it should be.

When personal sins are announced publicly, as in the case of the opening story, more harm than good is done. The pastor should have commended that young couple for their repentant spirit, exhorted them to be disciplined prior to the wedding and then encouraged them to enjoy God's wonderful forgiveness. Nothing pleasing to the Lord was accomplished by the public disclosure of that personal matter.

Confusing confessions

Confusing confessions are sometimes made during revival movements. One person may say to another, "I want you to forgive me for hating you these past five years!" But if the person was not aware of that hatred, private sin was unnecessarily confessed on a personal level. It is possible to despise someone in our minds while treating them outwardly with civility.

Congregations where personal, private and public sins are not being addressed properly will soon find themselves embroiled in numerous controversies. It is little wonder that fights are breaking out all over. So many sensitive issues are at stake, and "handle with care" cannot be overstated.

Quarrels often break out when confidentiality is broken in a counseling situation. One pastor shared the story of a couple he was counseling—"Paul and Pat." A lady in the church, "Joan," had referred this troubled couple to the minister. Pat had confided in Joan, and she dutifully reported it to her pastor so that he could have a ministry of healing in that home. So far, so good.

The pastor began to make significant

progress with Paul and Pat. It appeared that their home would be put back together by the grace of God. But Joan knew too much, and could not keep Pat's confidential confessions to herself. When it appeared that the minister was not going to relay all the juicy details of the couple's struggles to the church board, she decided to step in. The trouble began.

Soon the church knew the details about Paul and Pat and their marital problems. The public release of this private information formed a new wedge between the couple. Paul and Pat were divorced a year later. The pastor believes to this day that the marriage could have been saved. But Joan could not keep her treasured secrets to herself. Her sin destroyed a marriage.

When pastors sin

When ministers fail in moral or ethical matters, the response can lead to explosive consequences. People struggle with a variety of emotions when a man of the cloth falls into sin. They feel shocked and betrayed. Faith is shaken because that man up so high on the pedestal has suddenly plummeted so low.

Some are embarrassed while others are angered. Many wonder openly if the church will survive the sordid news of the leader's disgrace. A few may even be tempted to say, "I told you so." They sensed a fatal flaw in the preacher all along and thus were not really surprised when the story broke.

One church board began to keep a record of "little lies" their pastor had been telling. At one big showdown meeting, the list was presented. The pastor decided to resign during the confrontation. But when he abdicated his ministry a few weeks later, the congregation was appalled at the way in which the matter was handled. They were completely unaware of the minister's dishonesty and nothing was ever publicly explained. Some left the church while others from both sides debated for months after the pastor had moved to another state.

District leaders are often caught in the middle of these difficult disciplinary decisions. A leader must balance the need for unity and stability in the congregation with the importance of restoring God's fallen servant. Wherever possible, the district superintendent must help rescue both the people and the pastor. But if he does not find that vital equilibrium, hostility will soon turn to full scale war.

Christians will fail. It is our reaction to failure that will determine the relative peace or pugnacity in the church. It is more than obvious that many congregations have decided to respond to the believer's deficiency in an exaggerated, unscriptural manner. For sowing seeds of mishandled discipline, we have reaped congregations in conflict.

Lifestyles of the Proud and Powerful

I've gotten rid of six pastors before you came, and I can get rid of you, too! Those are the exact words of an elder from a church in the South. This sentence followed some choice curse words aimed at the minister after a disagreement one day. He just wanted to make sure that the preacher clearly understood who was in charge.

Welcome to the show *Lifestyles of the Proud and Powerful*. It is a daily drama airing in many cities across the land. The leading characters are sometimes pastors, sometimes parishioners, and sometimes, both. Much like one would find on television, there are devious plots, subplots and power plays. There is mystery and intrigue. In the intense pursuit for domination, the performers will stop at nothing to win. Only the church loses.

Corporate invasion

One dangerous trend that has created these power plays in church life today is the subtle shift from "congregation" to "corporation." Pastors are interviewed and evaluated, and hired and fired like employees for IBM. Their daily and weekly use of time is carefully monitored and evaluated. Ministers are not yet punching a time clock, but that may come.

Some profound differences come into play when the church switches into the power-driven corporate genre. Instead of asking whether a pastor has "God's call" to be in a particular congregation, lay leaders today inquire about the businessman's bottom line: results. If he has demonstrated "success" in terms of church growth numerically and financially, the minister is regarded as the "right man for the job." But when the pastor can no longer produce the numbers, the power brokers will find a way to remove and replace him . . . "A.S.A.P."

The same holds true for assistant pastors and other staff members. These people are "hired" to do a certain job, and if they do not deliver on their job description, they may be quickly supplanted. The emphasis is on results over relationships, and management over ministry. Produce or pack your bags.

Just who are these new power brokers who have led this invasion of corporation into congregation? They are sometimes businessmen and women who have been carefully trained in secular professions to seek success at any cost to personnel. They care more about production than people. Their motto: "Not by the Spirit, but by my might and power, saith the boss."

I remember hearing a businessman say of his pastor, "We are not getting very much of a 'bang for our buck' out of this guy!" I cannot immediately recall the location of that principle in God's Word, but some church board members behave as if it were right up there with John 3:16. The preacher must "deliver," "earn his salary" and "produce."

Pastors who control

Some pastors are guilty of constructing their own empire instead of building the kingdom of God. They simply must have complete control. This kind of minister wants to oversee each committee to make sure that no one is opposing him or his plan for the church. He is careful to assure his support before a board meeting, so that the vote is guaranteed in his favor. This is a pastor constantly looking out for his competition or a *coup d'etat*.

One pastor said, "Every member of my board is someone I've personally led to Christ, and I've never had trouble with them. I held one man in my arms as he went through delirium tremens. Now he's on my board, and I can count on his vote. He owes me."

This passion for power among preachers and the laity has created an atmosphere for anarchy. Churches today are driven by dark, hidden, carnal forces into innumerable and unnecessary conflicts. Too many are grabbing the steering wheel at the same time and the result is a congregation headed for a collision.

Voting-block cliques

Rather than sticks of dynamite, we have cliques of dynamite. These are little groups of people that form strong voting blocks in the congregation. These corrupt clusters can impose their will on every major decision in the church. They often align themselves against the pastor or an opposing throng. This troublesome band is aware of and relishes the power they can wield in the affairs of the fellowship.

If a clique like this goes unchecked, it will eventually arrest control of the agenda. God's plan will take a back seat to what the power group has decided. A minister may be dismissed, demoted or ignored. One senior pastor told of how a small band of people persuaded the entire governing board to cut his salary, move him to a smaller parsonage and elevate another staff member above him—all in an effort to force his resignation. More disturbing than the evil of this betrayal was the assumption of clique members that they were doing God a favor.

Representative or congregational rule

Another volatile mix for misunderstanding is the clash between representative and congregational rule in a church. The representative style of church government is one where the congregation has elected representatives from the fellowship to give leadership and direction to the church. Thus, the governing or executive board makes the decisions based on input from the people.

The congregational system of church management relies on the entire congregation to render various verdicts. The whole church, for instance, would directly vote for the dismissal of the old pastor or the approval of a new one. They may even choose together the color scheme of a sanctuary or bathroom for the new building.

Power struggles are frequently produced when these two approaches confront each other in the same church. When the congregational-style person begins to attend the representative-style church, he or she will complain about "that small group of people who make all the decisions around here!" The "representative style" parishioner might gripe about "the whole church voting on every little thing." It becomes an argument over the proper distribution of authority, and the exchange is often heated.

Control fueled by failure

The desire for domination in the congregation is often fueled by the failure to be in control at home or in the work place. The frustrated lower level executive might consider the church governing board an easy target for venting his penchant for power. The pastor who is failing in family management may want to prove his worth by embracing an autocratic leadership style in his ministry. This kind of preacher often becomes a workaholic in an effort to hide from difficult, unresolved issues in his home.

Success can also lead to the abuse of power. Some prosperous businessmen have the notion that they can apply their corporate savvy to the matters of church government. People are hesitant to challenge such leaders because they hold eminent jobs, drive big cars and live in large homes. Unfortunately, the presence or absence of Christlikeness in the lives of these notable executives is rarely an issue. The fact that they get the job done and earn lots of money becomes their ticket for clout in the congregation.

Trapped by the wealthy

Becoming beholden to wealthy, powerful people is a typical trap into which young ministers fall. It often begins with a simple thing like a handshake on Christmas Sunday—a $50 bill is brushed into the pastor's palm. An offer for a better car or a larger home may follow. Promises of large donations for building projects are made. These individuals are often the very ones who used their clout to secure the pastor's call to that church.

However, it soon becomes evident that these favors have subtle strings attached. Before long, certain expectations develop in the relationship with these influential leaders. It often begins in innocence, but eventually the courtesies are unmasked as a mere ploy for power and leverage. When the pastor refuses to play the game, his days may be numbered. These commanding persons not only want a voice in the church—they vie for a loud, domineering role. Some have succeeded in buying themselves just that.

In the light of James 2:1–13, it is astounding that congregations continue to bow before the rich and powerful. After thousands of confirmations of this text throughout church history, one would think the body of Christ would have learned its lesson. "Is it not the rich who are exploiting you?" James says. Very few seem to have listened to our Lord's brother.

Christ gave us fair warning, too. The lifestyle of the proud and powerful is nothing new. Two thousand years ago a band of 12 men gathered around Jesus for the answer to what they thought was the ultimate question: "Who is the greatest?" (Mark 9:33–37). Knowing the hearts of human beings, our Lord was not surprised that they should ask. But He had a shocking answer.

"If anyone wants to be first, he must be the very last, and the servant of all," said the Savior (verse 35).

Perhaps they thought He would go down the list of 12, pointing out their strengths and weaknesses, and then narrow it down to the five top finalists. Next, Christ would explain how it could have been easy to select any one of those five as "the greatest." And then . . . after much prayer and consideration, the winner is . . .

How disappointed they must have been to discover that their Master had not even been preparing a ballot or a grade card! It was a jolting realization that power and greatness mean something entirely different within the kingdom of God. The dictionary of Deity had drastically altered this world's definitions.

> You know that the rulers of the Gentiles lord it over them, and their high officials exercise authority over them. Not so with you. Instead, whoever wants to become great among you must be your servant, and whoever wants to be first must be your slave—just as the Son of Man did not come to be served, but to serve, and to give his life as a ransom for many. (Matthew 20:25–28)

This startling teaching should have forever banished the problem of power games in the true church. But the carnal nature has gained the upperhand over the Christ nature in many believers. This cruel, self-centered, power-hungry trait of fallen man has rendered many congregations impotent in the face of enormous spiritual need throughout society. The result: too many leaders and not enough followers.

To Grow or Not to Grow

I t is very difficult to have a growing church in a community like ours."

"This is a rural setting, and we just don't expect to see church growth."

"Our attendance has been increasing for awhile, but now we feel that we need to consolidate the newcomers and emphasize discipleship for the believers."

"Our building is comfortably full right now and we just don't have the room or desire to expand. And besides, building costs are so high!"

"We don't want to become one of those big, impersonal churches."

"Our folks are afraid that if we get any larger we won't be able to know everyone."

These are some of the statements which help draw the battle lines between those who desire church growth and those who oppose it. Some fierce fighting is breaking out over this issue today. We have highly motivated individuals in our congregations who push for rapid expansion. Others urge patience and caution. This oil and water mixture of personalities does not usually flow together smoothly.

This tussle over "to grow or not to grow" has recently hit many communities that were once considered to be rural areas of the country. These are communities that used to be a safe distance from the large cities. But now, the rapidly paced expansion of the suburbs has changed forever some of these sleepy little hamlets almost overnight.

Suddenly, there are new neighbors and neighborhoods to be reached with the gospel. That "little country church" is being surrounded with numerous subdivisions. Farmland has given way to tree-lined cul-de-sacs with three bedroom homes and underground electricity. No one could have ever predicted the magnitude of this demographic shift in the population. This should be the kind of problem every congregation would want to have.

So why would someone not want to see their church grow? Could there be a connection between the "proud and powerful" mentality described in chapter eight and the resistance to enlargement? Indeed there is.

Decentralization of power

It becomes obvious that along with church expansion will come a greater decentralization of power. To put it bluntly, more people will mean less influence for the power brokers. This is why many groups stay small and ineffective. Any talk of growth is a threat to those who want to keep the church at a manageable number. They have seen the enemy, and it is a larger congregation.

Pastors who come to town expecting and encouraging the church to grow may be in for a real surprise. As new people begin to join the fellowship, there will be some unhappy long-time attenders. The poor excuses cited in the introduction to this chapter will come tumbling down in board meetings. Those in the power clique will begin to express resentment because they have been ignored in favor of the newcomers. "I used to know everybody here," they will say in mournful tones. But this is frequently a cover-up for the real concern—more people, less power . . . more converts, less clout.

Resistant to change

Many parishioners are simply at peace with the present. The very notion of change is repulsive to them. "We have reached a comfortable size and we like the friendliness of our little group." Newcomers will find themselves shut out.

This attitude could be compared to a group of friends that form on a college campus. A friendly dynamic has been achieved in the clique. Anyone added to that group could throw off the sense of balance that has been cultivated. Change through either addition to or subtraction from the gang is an unpleasant thought.

"We're not up to the challenge of changing things around here" seems to be the sentiment in many churches.

Rest from the rat race

Many see the house of the Lord as a refuge from the fast-paced lifestyle they feel forced into during the other six days of the week. They hear the call of Christ to "Come unto me and I will give you rest." And the church should be the place where they can go to get away from societal pressures.

After hearing "do this," "build that," "expand here," "improve there" all week at work, many do not want to be bothered on Sunday with more high-pressure growth talk. They have come to relax, to lay their burden down and to find solitude and inner peace. These folks are in no mood to hear Reverend Jones turn up the heat on the latest outreach program or fund-raising drive for the new sanctuary.

Finances and faith

Some people who oppose enlargement are keeping one eye on the church's monthly financial statement, and another eye on their own pocketbook. It is clear to them that expansion will be expensive. It would be costly in terms of faith to believe God for mortgage payments on that new building. Greater demands will be placed on everyone to give even more in the weekly offerings.

The vision for growth often fades into oblivion because of this kind of cold calculation. "Here's our present income, and here's what we would need to pay the mortgage. It can't be done, even if we raise a significant amount of cash first." The dream dies because of a lack of faith, finances or both.

Pastors on the move

Perhaps this is a key reason why pastors move on to another church: the conflict surrounding the resistance to growth. Things go well for the first few years. People are saved, and the congregation begins to grow. Then the dreaded "B" word is introduced—BUILD. From that moment on, the gauntlet has been thrown down. Fearful of deeper spiritual and financial commitments, many begin to look for a way out. The easiest solution seems to be a pastoral change. And so, a scheme is devised for the pastor's ouster.

After the minister has been duly dismissed, the part of the congregation that enjoyed his ministry and applauded the growth is left to squabble with the lynch mob. Some will leave in protest, while others stay behind to fight the anti-growth movement. Much too often, the next pastor comes in and this sinister cycle repeats itself all over again.

A minister on the West Coast confirmed this pattern. A few months after he assumed a new pastorate, he discovered the dismal truth about his three predecessors. All of them had been "fired" by the board right at the time when the church was once again growing.

Given the community and surroundings, it was a church that should have expanded at a rapid rate. But a tiny band of disgruntled leaders made sure that never happened. Through the years, they maintained control by keeping the fellowship small. These carnal men had achieved their goal, much to the offense of Christ Himself.

Manipulative tactics

Some who desperately want to see church growth are also subject to unspiritual motivation and manipulative tactics. There are those people who want expansion for its own sake. They see their fellowship as being in competition with other congregations in town, and they are driven to win the award for the largest church. And should they achieve that goal, they would not hesitate to take the credit for the success.

The individuals who express a passion for "church growth at any cost" can become as dangerous as the ones who would hold a congregation back from enlargement. They will criticize the cautious person as being weak and faithless. They may be constantly harassing the pastor for his lack of fire and vision. These people can become overbearing and obnoxious in their attempts to challenge the body of Christ to greater growth.

A pastor may become a menace in his over-zealous obsession with increased size. Subtle comments are made from the pulpit aimed at those who oppose expansion. Home visits become tainted with ulterior motives to convince more families that there really is a need for that new sanctuary. Parishioners begin to question the real reason behind this powerful push for greater numbers and larger buildings. Will the church become a monument to the greatness of God or will it become a memorial to the minister himself?

The most common scenario, however, is this: the pastor becomes mediator for a feuding flock that is sharply divided over the growth issue. The minister is frequently content to simply allow enlargement to occur naturally. He may see it as an inherent result of a faithful, full-orbed ministry. But the man of the cloth may find that his fabric is being pulled in two different directions by the opposing groups.

If he can bring the two sides together and work out a compromise, nurture and expansion can enjoy an equal emphasis in the church. If he cannot get these factions to meet and talk, both a split and the pastor's resignation may be imminent.

No either/or proposition

Like so many other things, "to grow or not to grow," to nurture the flock or to evangelize, is not an either/or proposition. Both emphases are scriptural and indispensable in a healthy church. Our bent toward the "pendulum complex" tends to sway us from one extreme to the other. But we must have indoctrination along with increase. It is most definitely a both/and scenario.

It is difficult to imagine IBM or GM employees fighting over whether or not they should expand their business base. Can you envision a conversation like this among corporate executives:

"Well, Jim, I just don't know. I realize that we can purchase the extra land at a bargain, but I like the size of the group of employees we have right now. We have developed that warm family feeling. I don't want to have to get to know a whole new gang of people in a larger facility."

"But Frank, think about the increased profits and productivity! We will be able to accomplish so much more if we will just expand this facility. Besides, someone else may get our customers if they see that we are going to reside in our comfort zone."

"You've made some good points, Jim. I still

need to think about it though. I like things just the way they are right now."

It sounds so silly. We can only guess how many minutes men or women like this would remain employed by their companies. But somehow, these altercations make sense to many people in the church of Jesus Christ. Few seem to be offended with the ludicrous act of debating the issues of growth and discipleship.

The Tongue Also Is a Fire

A pastor shared this most incredible story with me many years ago, and I have not been able to forget it. The pastor, "Jim," was visiting his parents in Evansville, Indiana. Jim and his parents attended the Sunday evening service at the local church. The minister of that church, "Dr. Spring" had been a friend of Jim's during seminary.

Dr. Spring recognized Jim in the audience with his parents and asked him to lead in prayer. Jim sensed tension and turmoil in the atmosphere from the very first moments of the service. Only one person came forward during the invitation that night out of an audience of several hundred. Something seemed wrong somewhere.

After the service, a young man, "Tom," shook hands with Jim. Tom told Jim that he was going into the ministry, and he mentioned how much he had appreciated Jim's prayer during the service. The next morning, Tom called Jim at his parents' home. What he was about to say left Jim speechless at the other end of the telephone line.

"I felt led of God to ask you to pray with me and a group in the church. We are praying for our pastor—we have evidence that he is a drug addict."

Jim was invited to Tom's home, and the overwhelming curiosity of the situation urged him to meet with Tom. A few hours later, Jim arrived at Tom's home, and was introduced to a "Dr. White"—the former pastor of the church. For two hours, these two men tried to convince Jim that Dr. Spring was a drug addict.

After Dr. White left, Jim expressed doubts about the wild accusations. "I do not believe that Dr. Spring is involved with drugs. But I need to confront him with these charges. If this is true, he desperately needs help. If it is not true, Dr. Spring must be made aware of this vicious scandal that could ruin his ministry."

Jim went the next day to talk with Dr. Spring. After detailing all of the charges, the minister began to frantically pace the floor. Dr. Spring then put his hands on Jim's shoulders, looked him straight in the eye, and said, "Jim, I am a dedicated Christian. I have never used drugs of any kind other than ones any person could readily obtain over the counter at a pharmacy. But your conversation with me today is helping me to put some things together in my mind. Will you meet with me and the other parties at my lawyer's office tomorrow?" Jim nodded in agreement. Time and location were established.

Finally, everyone met together with Dr. Spring and his lawyer: the area superintendent for the denomination, "Dr. Hutchinson," Tom, Dr. White and Jim. The attorney went around the circle and asked each man what evidence he had to support the charge of drug addiction. Tom began to cry. "I don't have any proof that would stand up in court, but Dr. White told me about our pastor's problem with drugs."

Dr. White, turning the color of his name, turned to Dr. Hutchinson, saying, "The superintendent told me." Dr. Hutchinson, looking extremely nervous and pale, admitted that one of the bishops shared the story with him.

Dr. Spring seized a dramatic moment of silence by saying, "I categorically deny having ever used drugs, and I am willing to go to any hospital in Indianapolis for a thorough examination." The three accusers agreed that this would be a good way to resolve the matter.

The minister was examined by four doctors. They unanimously agreed that there was not the slightest evidence that Dr. Spring had ever been a drug addict. Shortly after this report was filed, Dr. Hutchinson asked both Dr. Spring and the whole church to forgive him and the others who had perpetrated this terrible lie.

Later, Dr. Spring wrote to Jim to say that they

had traced the gossip back to a camp meeting in Lakeland, Florida, some 20 years before. Dr. Spring was preaching a sermon when he suddenly fainted and collapsed. Apparently, one minister said to another that he "wondered" if Dr. Spring was using drugs. "I heard about a minister that fainted during his message, and they later discovered that he was hooked on drugs," he said. That preacher told the next one with added innuendo, and so on. It was not long before the story was that "Dr. Spring has a problem with drug addiction."

No one ever had the courage or love to confront Dr. Spring directly with this charge. This accusation undermined his ministry in four churches over a span of 20 years. Though he later received a letter of apology signed by the whole board of bishops for that denomination, the damage had been done. Dr. Spring had suffered the irreparable destruction of his good name.

Kindled by a small flame

James 3:3–8 reminds us just how much wood can be kindled by a small flame. The small ember can become a firefighter's nightmare in minutes. The New English Bible translates it: "What an immense stack of timber can be set ablaze by the tiniest spark!"

"The tongue also is a fire." The writer unveils a parallel portrait of devastation that the tongue can deliver. Like the fierce, uncontrollable wildfires of the forest, this "little member" can spread discord and disaster everywhere it goes. "A scoundrel repeats evil gossip; it is like a scorching fire on his lips" (Proverbs 16:27, NEB).

"The tongue is . . . a world of iniquity." James indicates that the tongue is a vast system or network that is tied in with iniquity. No other part of our body has comparable power or range of influence for the kingdom of darkness. From the tongue can come the utterance of every evil thought and motive. The feelings of others can be slashed to pieces by the reckless, ruthless tongue.

Many divorces are prompted and promoted by the hateful communication spewed forth from the tongue. The spoken word, inspired by this fiery world of iniquity, has sewn discord and separation in multitudes of families. "As charcoal to embers and as wood to fire,/ so is a quarrelsome man for kindling strife" (Proverbs 26:21).

Gossip corrupts

Gossip has corrupted thousands of churches. Battered by bitterness and slander, many congregations have split right down the middle. Some have disintegrated entirely because of the damage inflicted by vicious tongues. The godly character of ministers, church board members and other lay people has been maligned if not mangled by ill-founded rumor and innuendo.

I could never forget one of my own experiences as a pastor. One of my elders came to our house on a Sunday afternoon. He was haunted by hearsay and completely distraught. My wife and I were shocked at the things that had been said behind our backs. The elder had indicated that it appeared to be a widespread problem. "We will see about that," I said.

That evening after the service, I gathered the gossipers in my office. As it turned out, there were only two who were actually involved with this rumor mill. Upon being confronted, they both admitted that they had no basis for their criticism. Each one offered to ask the congregation's forgiveness in a public service. Since their bitterness had "sprung up to trouble many," I agreed to let them confess their sin in this manner.

That was a real turning point in the life, health and growth of that church. At the next board meeting, I poured my heart out to the leadership. My request was a simple one: please talk *to* me . . . not *about* me. This was a cleansing time that led to a period of unprecedented growth.

Congregations are in conflict because "the tongue also is a fire, a world of evil" (James 3:6a). Oh, the potential danger, the powerful damage that can result from the untamed tongue: "It is a restless evil, full of deadly poison" (3:8).

11

The Drinking Dilemma

The National Association of Student Councils Convention in 1988 was attended by 1,154 delegates. These were high school students elected by their peers to serve in local student government positions. Meeting in Albuquerque, New Mexico, these teenagers represented both public and private schools from all 50 states, Washington, D.C. and Puerto Rico.

USA Today polled this broad representation of young people and discovered some shocking statistics related to teens and alcohol. When asked if they knew students who drank beer at least once a week, 63 percent of these student leaders said yes. Even more alarming was the admission by 47 percent of them who knew peers who used liquor weekly. Only 25 percent knew those who were smoking marijuana, and nine percent could name those who were doing cocaine or crack. (June 28, 1988, p. 1A)

The poll seems to indicate a trend away from "hard drugs" to what is perceived to be a "soft drug," namely alcohol. Top athletes and famous movie stars have died very tragic, highly visible, drug-related deaths in recent years. This has served as a warning. Today's teens are shifting their allegiance to beer, wine and hard liquor. It is presumed to be a "safer high."

Society is also struggling with rampant adult alcoholism. Kitty Dukakis stunned the nation when her obsession with drinking led to a shot glass of rubbing alcohol. Many other famous politicians and actors have been checking in to places like the Betty Ford Clinic. A rising number of drunk-driver homicides led to the formation of M.A.D.D.—Mothers Against Drunk Driving. Increasing domestic violence is often considered to be alcohol-aggravated.

Social drinking

While this has been happening in the world, the church has been trying to cope with what David Wilkerson calls, "sipping saints." Though no evangelical Christian would advocate drunkenness, there seems to be an increasing number of believers who feel strongly that "social drinking" is a personal matter that should not be subject to sermonic sanctions.

During a crusade in the western United States, a pastor expressed a rather passive position on this subject. "How do you handle the social drinking issue out here?" I inquired.

"Well, Tom, I just don't mention it at all. Too

many of my people enjoy a beer or a little wine once in a while."

I have discovered that this is indeed a "hot button" in many congregations. It appears to be somewhat of an "older generation vs. younger generation" dispute, with younger couples today taking a very liberal, casual approach.

The key conflict centers around two words: abstinence and moderation. One group believes in total abstinence—that under no circumstances should a Christian drink any kind of alcoholic beverage. The other side says that moderation is the real issue—believers should be free to drink anything as long as they remain in control. For instance, they would point to Ephesians 5:18, and say, "Paul said that we are not to get DRUNK on wine. . . . He did NOT say that we should never drink wine!"

The tea-totaler would argue that it is a matter of testimony. "Younger Christians, who may not be aware of your personal discipline, might stumble because of your bad example. What you may be able to do in moderation, others could carry to excess."

The sipping saint would reply that the younger believer should be taught the importance of tolerance through all of this. "There will be many issues that place good, godly people on opposite sides, and it is good for the babe in Christ to learn how to cope with this early on."

Was it Welch's?

Did Jesus turn water into wine or Welch's grape juice in John 2:1–11? This makes for an interesting debate. The abstinence advocate prefers the latter translation. Christ wanted the guests to have a pure drink of grape juice. And besides, the regular drinking water was often contaminated in those days, so our Lord had to turn it into something safe for consumption!

Others see it differently. They understand the wine from the wedding at Cana to be an alcoholic beverage, though admittedly some of the wine was stronger than the rest. "Everyone brings out the choice wine first and then the cheaper wine after the guests have had too much to drink" (John 2:10). Was Jesus alluding to an overdose of grape juice? Hardly, says the sipping saint. Through some eyes, Christ is endorsing the use of fermented wine at a time of celebration.

The prohibition of several Proverbs has heated up many conversations between opposing forces in the beverage wars. "Wine is a mocker and beer a brawler; whoever is led astray by them is not wise" (Proverbs 20:1). It is the phrase "led astray" that leads to further debate and dissention. One side sees a general overtone of decadence inherent in being "led astray."

The other group believes that it is a matter of degrees. "It is possible to be led astray by wine and beer if you drink until you're drunk . . . but in moderation, these beverages can be as innocent as water or a soft drink."

Former alcoholics are often the most ardent advocates of total abstinence. They know firsthand the danger and damage of being drunk with beer, wine and liquor. These people often feel compelled to crusade against any use of alcoholic drinks whatsoever. In their great zeal, they may become overbearing. Other believers, who have never had a "control problem," find it difficult to relate to the doom and gloom prophecies of the detoxified drunk. This can become a dramatic clash of wills.

Cultural practice

Some Christians come from a background where beer drinking and wine sipping were just a part of normal living. No one got drunk. These beverages were enjoyed for their acquired taste, and usually accompanied a meal. It was no big deal to them before they came to Christ, and it is no big deal to them now. Such individuals are confused with all the fuss. To them, it is as senseless as an argument about whether one prefers Pepsi or Coke. They make no attempt to hide bottles or cans because they feel they have nothing for which to be ashamed.

European believers are particularly immune

to the notion of abstinence. To these Christians, communion just would not be communion without real wine. Visitors are routinely offered wine along with dinner in the evening. It is a "non-issue" in most European evangelical homes and churches. Missionaries from the United States and Canada often find themselves wrestling with the social and societal implications of total abstinence. Just what did Paul mean when he said to be "all things to all people?" Should we condemn their custom if it has not led to debauchery?

A pastor can find himself in awkward situations with sipping saints. He may suddenly discover that one of his governing board members, duly elected by the congregation, has the occasional beer or glass of wine. What if the minister confronts that leader privately and senses no remorse or willingness to change? Will it have to be brought before the elders or the entire board? Is that pastor prepared for the possibility that the whole church may become embroiled in colossal combat over social drinking?

Recently, a minister in whose church I was crusading was considering his options for dealing with this very dilemma. A teenager in the church had begun to drink occasionally, and when confronted with the evidence, he said, "So what? There's nothing wrong with having a couple of drinks! Besides, I've seen some of the leaders of this church drinking wine and beer at a restaurant!"

The pastor found out that the young man was telling the truth. Now he must find a way to lovingly confront those who were identified. He is struggling with this question: "Just what is the accountability of a church leader to the adults and young people of the congregation?"

Abstinence documents

Denominations are rushing abstinence documents to the printer in an effort to stem the tide of broadminded ministers who are ordained in their fellowship. For most fundamental, evangelical groups, tea-totaling has been an unwritten rule among the clergy for many years. That is no longer a safe assumption. If pressed on the issue, many pastors today would fight for their right to control their own belief and behavior in the matter of social drinking.

This particular form of congregational conflict tends to have a long fuse. It boils and bubbles up a little here and then a little there. It goes away for awhile, then returns, only to go away again. The social drinking question seethes with subtleties and cruises with caution. Then, all at once, it explodes. Sides are chosen. Walls are erected. Hasty judgments are made. Feelings are hurt. Families are divided. Churches are split.

Does the Bible absolutely, undeniably teach us to totally abstain from drinking alcoholic beverages? Perhaps that is not even the right question. Maybe there are greater issues to be considered in this divisive debate. But one thing *IS* certain: we are absolutely, undeniably called to love one another in the midst of our differences. Conflict, of whatever kind, must be conquered by the grace and power of God. This much we can proclaim with certainty.

Charismaniacs and Charisphobics

Small groups began meeting to encourage a "deeper" study of the Bible and to promote a more "genuine" prayer life. At first, the pastor was unaware of these special gatherings. But the numbers began to grow to the point where everyone noticed. Curiosity became intense concerning the teachings and practices of these new clusters.

People began to talk about their new freedom in prayer and their better understanding of God's Word. Some began to minimize the importance of the Sunday services because they were so thrilled with their new extracurricular assembly. They had discovered a more complete Christian experience.

It eventually became clear that the church was being invaded by the forces of the charismatic movement. The "new freedom in prayer" turned out to be an emphasis on praying in tongues. The "better understanding of God's Word" was focused particularly on the book of Acts and certain chapters in First Corinthians. These Christians had experienced a new "baptism in the Spirit." They were now free to truly worship the Lord.

Questions, confusion and doubt arrested the atmosphere. The small group leaders insisted that they were not judging anyone. They were not teaching anything strange or heretical. "We just want God's people to experience all of the blessings of His Word," they said.

The pastor did his best to cope with the explosive situation. He met with the leaders of the charismatic cliques in an effort to find some common ground. Several key families were enchanted by the new teaching, and the minister was desperate to consolidate the congregation. But only so many compromises could be made.

The dynamic and popular Bible study leaders insisted that everyone in the church should enjoy the gift of tongues in their prayer life. Christians should be free to share prophecies and words of wisdom as the Spirit led in each service. The people of God should be free in the Lord to exercise their spiritual gifts.

All attempts by the minister to maintain an open mind came to an abrupt end. He did not question the need for God's people to practice their spiritual gifts. However, the insistence that *EVERYONE* pray or speak in tongues was the last straw. The pastor could see no scriptural justification for that position. He felt that God's Word clearly stated that the Holy Spirit distributes His gifts "severally, as He chooses" (1 Corinthians 12:11, KJV).

The church split left no one untouched. Families were cut apart by the division. Numerous people left the congregation to start a new fellowship that would be "free in the Spirit." The pastor remained for awhile to preside over the fractured flock. But one year after the split, he suddenly resigned and moved to another church.

If this story sounds unfamiliar to you, check your birth certificate for the name "Rip Van Winkle." You must have slept through a few decades of church history, namely the 1970s and 1980s. The charismatic movement has probably been the single most divisive element of the 20th century, but many teachings have just recently taken their greatest toll.

Three schools of thought

There are essentially three schools of thought concerning the gifts of the Spirit. Some denominations and churches would deny both the presence of and the need for spiritual gifts in the church today. These groups would say that all of this appropriately disappeared after the first century. They feel that the Holy Spirit was given in a special, one-time dispensation, to get the church off the ground. After that was accomplished, spiritual gifts were no longer essential to the daily life and operations of the church.

At the other end of the pendulum are those who would insist that all spiritual gifts are valid and operative for contemporary Christians. In varying degrees, these groups insist that the evidence of spiritual life is the gift of tongues. Some would say that it is the proof of salvation, where others would see it as an indication of having been "baptized" in the Spirit subsequent to salvation. Feelings run very strong in these fellowships concerning the importance of this one particular spiritual enabling—the gift of tongues.

Between the extremes

Between these two extreme viewpoints would be the third school of thought. Many denominations and churches believe in the relevance of spiritual gifts for the church today without emphasizing any particular gift. These congregations would not, for example, place any more importance on tongues than they would on the gift of wisdom or administration. They are content to allow the Holy Spirit to select the special enabling that each believer will need in his or her spiritual pilgrimage.

Someone has suggested that the three schools of thought can actually be reduced to two: the charismaniacs and the charisphobics. The terms are well chosen, and both speak volumes as to the heart of the controversy.

Charismaniacs can be overwhelming in their obsession with the more dramatic elements of spiritual life. They love to talk about a special "prayer language," and a word of "wisdom," "prophecy" or "knowledge." They speak of signs, wonders and "power encounters."

The pitfalls

As a pastor, I was always trying to understand the mentality of the charismaniac. I had lunch one day with an assistant pastor from a charismatic church in town. After a half hour of general conversation, I looked him right in the eye and asked what I considered to be the key question: "Can my preaching ministry be truly anointed by God's Spirit if I have never experienced the gift of tongues?"

He tried his best to be diplomatic and say that my preaching would certainly be enhanced if I would embrace "glossolalia" in my personal spiritual life. But the bottom line was exceedingly clear in his tone: his preaching would always be at a "deeper level" than mine because of his baptism in the Spirit as evidenced by the gift of tongues.

This is doubtless the most perilous pitfall of the charismaniac. This person often has a tendency to look down upon those who have not experienced God in the exact same manner as he or she has. Some of these people seem to thrive on the fact that others lack the faith and spiritual insight which they have. They see themselves as a cut above the average Christian.

On the other hand, the charisphobic has his or her own set of problems and prejudices. Though he or she may claim otherwise, this person often lacks a genuine openness to all that God may have for him or her. The charisphobic can be guilty of limiting the Lord, and is at risk of missing the full measure of spiritual blessing intended for him or her. This person's fear of the charismaniac and charismatic issues has the potential to keep him or her away from achieving genuine spiritual depth. The charisphobic is hesitant, if not entirely unwilling, to admit that he or she might actually be able to learn something from the charismatic believer.

Churches cracked wide open

Literally hundreds of churches have been cracked wide open in the past decades because of the charismatic controversy. New groups are splintering off here, there and everywhere in a frantic attempt to find real "freedom" in Christ. That quest for liberty, from both sides, has led us into the shackles of shameful combat.

Congregations are in conflict today because of our inability to embrace First Corinthians 13 right in the middle of chapters 12 and 14. The placement of the love passage is far from coincidental. Indeed, "the greatest of these *is* love."

Our unwillingness to cope with charismatic questions in the agape context has created an atmosphere which is ripe for a riot.

The church today has a very spurious translation of First Corinthians 14:40: "Let all things be done divisively and in chaos."

PART II

Results of Church Conflict

What consequences does the congregation in conflict face? There are at least five specific results delineated here in part two. Ponder these repercussions in relationship to your own church. Some may already be in evidence, while others are still developing. But this much is certain: there can be no church conflict without serious consequences. Eileen Wilmoth said this:

> Little schisms and contentions that occur behind the shiny appearance of the church are like the little hairline cracks that appear beneath the glaze of an inexpensive, much-used breakfast plate. One day under pressure, too much hot water, or rough handling, that plate will break. Likewise, unattended contentions in the church can damage the unity of its members and harm its witness to the world.

Our Purpose for Existence

The pilot calmly took the microphone. "Ladies and gentlemen, I am pleased to announce that we have reached our cruising altitude of 35,000 feet. However, I have some good news and some bad news. The bad news is that we have lost power in all of our navigational systems, and we don't know what direction we are going. The good news is that we are making record time."

The pilot did not want to concern his passengers with the consequences of this equipment failure. He chose to humor the listeners with the thought of a speedy journey.

So it is in many churches today. In the midst of our frequent fights, we have lost our sense of purpose and direction. But no one has time to care because we have learned to keep busy and dizzy in a flurry of activity. This temporarily soothes the soul and covers up the conflict. But eventually and appropriately the questions arise: "Why are we doing all this? What is the purpose of this church? Why are we here anyway?"

> My prayer is not for them alone. I pray also for those who will believe in me through their message, that all of them may be one, Father, just as you are in me and I am in you. May they also be in us so that the world may believe that you have sent me. I have given them the glory that you gave me, that they may be one as we are one: I in them and you in me. May they be brought to complete unity to let the world know that you sent me and have loved them even as you have loved me. (John 17:20–23)

Christ states the very purpose of our existence as a church in one crisp phrase: "To let the world know that you sent me and have loved them even as you have loved me"(verse 23). This is what it's all about. Our reason for being is summed up in this terse utterance. Local congregations are responsible to let the world know that Jesus is the "sent One," the Messiah, and that He deeply loves each member of the human race.

The purpose statement is preceded by three specific ways in which the church can fulfill this very objective:

1. The church must be in Christ (verse 21).

2. The church must be one with each other as Christ is one with God (verse 22).

3. The church must be brought to complete unity (verse 23).

If we are to accomplish the stated purpose of our Lord, we need to be "in Christ." The picture here is a congregation encompassed by the triune God ("may they also be in us . . . "). It is a fellowship that is covered and enveloped by the very presence and fragrance of deity.

If the world only sees "us," with all of our fights and failures, they will not be attracted to our message or our Master. Our congregations will be regarded as just another human enterprise, devoid of any special spiritual power or significance. And that is precisely the reputation some churches have today—a mere organization of people like a civic club.

What makes a church distinct?

What will make the local congregation distinct in the community? It will always and only be the fact that the church is "in Christ." It must not be into itself, into conflict or even into good programs and projects primarily. If we would fulfill Christ's purpose, that He be known as a loving Savior, we must dwell in the shadow of the Almighty. This, and this alone will captivate a fallen world with the loveliness of Christ.

But alas, society has witnessed our confusion and conflicts. People can rightfully point the finger and say that we have failed to show them the Savior because we are no longer hidden in Christ. We have stepped out from behind the safety of the cross in a feeble attempt to win a world through our clever techniques. But the hypocrisy of it all does not go unnoticed.

The second step

The second step to fulfilling our Lord's purpose for His church is to be "one with each other as Christ is one with God" (verse 22). The oneness of Jesus with His Father is the model to which the church must aspire if the world is to know that a loving Savior has been sent from God.

But those on the outside looking into our fellowships have more often seen our opposition to each other than our oneness with each other. Skeptical souls have heard us talk about how Christians are likeminded, but in actuality they have observed our cool distance from one another.

Being "brought to complete unity" is the third component "to let the world know that you sent me and have loved them even as you have loved me." United, we stand to proudly present our Savior to a needy world; divided, we fall in disgrace and fail to perform our purpose as a congregation.

This prayer of Jesus Christ strikes at the very heart of God's will for the church. Our Supreme Commander has spoken. He has a plan for the spread of the good news that Messiah has come. The Lord has chosen to use His church. But His people must reside in Him, they must be one with each other and they must be unified in the bond of mutual love.

For this reason the congregation in conflict is relegated to obscurity. It has no oneness, no unity, no sense of the enveloping presence of the Lord Jesus. Having lost its purpose for existence in the shuffle of the scuffle, this church is placed in hiding.

> Crowns and thrones may perish,
>   kingdoms rise and wane,
> But the church of Jesus hidden does
>   remain;
> Gates of hell should never 'gainst that
>   church prevail,
> We have Christ's own promise but think
>   that it will fail. (Verwer, p. 92)

God has His ways of secluding the skirmishing saints. In His great desire for the world to know about the coming of His Son, Jehovah can swiftly move to nullify the bad influences of contemptuous congregations. How sad it is to see those churches that once shined and shouted the good news now silenced by internal strife.

Society simply cannot know about the arrival of Jesus Christ or the love of God when local churches are fractured by fighting, consumed with conflict and battered with bitterness. Our message becomes meaningless when we are battling among ourselves.

Today's church needs to take a fresh look at its statement of purpose. We were not placed here to provide a forum for debate and dissension. Our congregations are here to demonstrate, through our love and unity, that "God so loved the world that he gave his one and only Son, that whoever believes in him shall not perish but have eternal life" (John 3:16).

Our Plausibility among Young People

He doesn't attend church anymore. "Bill" used to go regularly as a child and for awhile as a teenager. But now, as a college graduate and young husband, he struggles to find the time and the reasons for a Sunday drive to that brick building a few miles away. From time to time, he has even received friendly invitations from neighbors to join them at church. Bill finds it easy to come up with excuses.

In many ways, he was a typical young man in society. Bill had grown up in a small community, worshiping with his family in a small evangelical congregation. He faithfully attended Sunday school and church services. Becoming active in the youth group, Bill spent many hours with other teens in the congregation.

But Bill's church had a reputation for fighting

throughout his formative years. Pastors only lasted an average of two years in this fractured fellowship. There was even a sense of sinister pride among the parishioners for their skill in moving preachers around. Some kind of conflict was always brewing. The atmosphere was consistently charged with "wars and rumors of wars."

This steady diet of infighting took its toll on Bill's faith. At one time, he would have claimed to have a personal relationship with the Lord, but he doubts all of that now. Like so many, Bill has become disillusioned by dissension in the body of Christ. He wants to believe the Bible, but the unrelenting hypocrisy of "Christians" in his past haunts him.

Bill doesn't attend church anymore. He is a casualty of war—a direct result of a congregation's failure to even remotely resemble the ideals of God's Word. Though his excuses will not serve him well in the ultimate court of Christ Jesus the Lord, Bill's disenchantment casts its own judgment on that local congregation.

The combative church risks losing its plausibility among young people. That which is plausible is "something that seems valid or likely reliable." And young people are carefully looking for evidence to validate the reliability of the Christian faith.

Young people are watching

Youthful eyes and ears are wide open each week as the congregation gathers for worship. They watch and they listen. These young folks frequently appear to have little or no reaction to the chaos in the congregation. Nevertheless, they are taking note of the fact that Sunday school lessons and memorized Scripture verses regularly clash with the attitudes and actions seen in the routines of church life.

> Encourage the young men to be self-controlled. In everything set them an example by doing what is good. In your teaching show integrity, seriousness and soundness of speech that cannot be condemned, so that those who oppose you may be ashamed because they have nothing bad to say about us. (Titus 2:6–8)

The Apostle underlines our critical need to be an example to impressionable young people. Paul places "doing what is good" before "teaching with integrity, seriousness, and soundness of speech." In both "walk" and "talk," older Christians are responsible to lead younger Christians by a righteous, respectable lifestyle.

Teaching that is sound and serious will be devoid of the sarcasm and contempt that laces so many conversations among Christians today. Our casual approach to solemn matters of eternal life and death can bear only negative fruit in the next generation.

The congregation in conflict so quickly forgets those little eyes and ears that see and hear so accurately. While calloused adults carelessly fight it out, the younger ones are at first confused; later, they become disillusioned. They may leave the church altogether and not even attempt to find a replacement. Or these confusd parishioners might give it one more try in another congregation.

One thing is certain: God's people have a strong desire to worship in an atmosphere of peace and loving fellowship. Most believers will not put up with petty disputes for any length of time. If they sense that a pattern for pugnacity has been established, they will soon be on their way.

This is why many churches are left with a small nucleus of the original "prize fighters." Congregations once mighty with young couples, families and teenagers are eventually reduced to the remnants of the rabble rousers. Too many cold, gray, stormy days of conflict prompted them to seek the warmth and sunshine offered in other churches.

Keen perception

We have underestimated the broad talents of perception that reside within our young people. They are more aware of our heated debates and hypocrisy than we could imagine. Our internal strife cannot be comfortably stored away in secrecy. There is really nowhere to hide our quarrels. Unpleasant though true, the youth group probably knows more than it cares to know about the latest controversy.

Obviously, there is no perfect church. No one would seriously suggest that we diligently search for the flawless congregation. That group is nowhere to be found. However, our young people and young couples have a right to see church conflict resolved in a scriptural, serene manner. Though there are and will be strong disagreements between believers, there are also correct, Christlike solutions.

This may be one of the most attractive aspects of genuine Christianity. The Bible does not portray the believer's sojourn as pie in the sky—sometimes, it's pie in the face! But that face can be wiped completely clean and we can experience the joy of a fresh start. Trials and questions will arise. Some difficulties will require time, patience and much prayer. But in a world of uncertainty, the church can boldly announce that Christ has the answer to our most complex dilemmas.

Continuous conflict denies God's power

The congregation that is continually in conflict implies that they have problems even the Lord Himself cannot solve. This provides the worst possible role model for young people who already have enough temptations to doubt and despair. These young men and women must know the answer to the question posed in Genesis 18:14, "Is anything too hard for the Lord?"

If you are searching for a reason to resolve your church conflict, look no further than your church youth group. Our Christian example must be plausible before it can be applicable in young lives. Adults may choose to play carnal games in their congregation, but the next generation may choose not to play at all.

One of the great results of the Canadian revival of 1971 was the new attitude among the young people when they saw the sincerity of their parents. After meeting separately one night, the next evening they reported, "We'd rather be with the adults. Since they've quit playing church and are honest with God, we want to be with them—right where the action is." (Lutzer, p. 34)

Our Potential for Growth

A famous evangelist once said to a group of pastors, "Gentlemen, some of you are just a few funerals away from church growth!"

Obviously, it is not always the older folks who cause conflict in a congregation. Nevertheless, the point is made just the same. It would seem that some people must either leave the church or die before true peace can be restored and growth can be revived. This is another hard and fast ministry "fact of life."

> Then the church throughout Judea, Galilee, and Samaria enjoyed a time of peace. It was strengthened; and encouraged by the Holy Spirit, it grew in numbers, living in the fear of the Lord. (Acts 9:31)

This verse is loaded with characteristics of the growing church. The flourishing congregation can be identified by four attributes:

1. An atmosphere of peace.

2. A dedication to become stronger.

3. The encouragement of the Holy Spirit.

4. A willingness to maintain a reverential fear of the Lord.

Any group of God's people that will launch out in these four directions will discover that their fellowship will expand.

A dramatic contrast can be seen in the combative congregation. "Peace, peace," its members cry, but there is no peace. They are concentrating on their weaknesses rather than focusing on strengths. The Holy Spirit's convicting, comforting presence is ignored in such a fellowship, and they do indeed behave in a manner that denies any real fear of God. This is a dependable recipe for producing the incredible shrinking church.

Dwell on any declining congregation that comes to your mind. Perhaps you are forced to think about the one you are now pastoring or attending. You will discover that there is a direct correlation between the years of struggle and strife and those plummeting attendance records. This is true regardless of location or denomination.

It is no mere coincidence that the first century church "enjoyed a time of peace" and simultaneously "grew in numbers." The two principles go hand in hand.

Asleep in Zion

A church may be able to forge a peace without growth. I have visited many congregations whose members are quite content to record the same basic numbers year after year. They have modeled their fellowship after a mutual admiration society. "Us four and no more" is their comfortable creed.

That church exists in terms of a building and a parking lot. It has an address and telephone number in the yellow pages. But this group is asleep in Zion, content to play the fiddle while humanity teeters on the brink of hellfire. Many plateaued congregations have settled for this pseudo-peace without growth.

But there cannot be church growth without peace. Harmony is an indispensable quality for the expanding fellowship. A settled, serene, secure atmosphere may be the most attractive asset of a group that is poised for enlargement. Visitors, both churched and unchurched, will be drawn into the calm, controlled environment of the parish at peace.

As we have witnessed the meltdown of the iron curtain, there is much talk of a "peace dividend" for both communistic and democratic nations. The notion is that as swords are converted into plowshares, there will be less money needed for waging a third world war. More funds will be available for our staggering domestic needs.

There are "peace dividends" for the church that will lay down its guns, too. As the people of God resolve their disputes, we can then direct our energies toward the twin necessities of discipleship and evangelism. When our focus is no longer forced to be inward, coping with internal conflict, we can be free to reach outward to communities that are ready and waiting.

New members become referees

It is interesting to be a guest at someone else's family reunion. If a feud is brewing, often the outsider is called in to act as a "referee." This is a most uncomfortable assignment, and most of us would avoid it like an extra hour of choir practice. The guest is placed in a no-win, awkward situation. He or she will soon be looking for the exit.

That is precisely what happens when visitors are thrown into the middle of our church family conflicts. Before they even know a few names, the newcomers are courted by both sides of the disputing factions. Not wanting to hurt anyone's feelings in particular, they usually just look for the door and move on in their quest for a church that they can call "home."

We should not pillow our conscience with the silly idea that those who visit our fellowships cannot feel our malcontent. In fact, guests seem to have a "sixth sense" about them. Though it may be true that we can cover up for awhile, we will not fool the visitor for any period of time. Our true colors—black and blue—will eventually show through.

Could we estimate the number of people on any given Sunday who must go full circle in the revolving door of a congregation consumed with contention? The figure would doubtless be shocking. What a tragedy to see churches that fritter away their potential for expansion because of internal bickering. Pastors have said to me, "I see many visitors come in our front door and get out that back door just as quickly as they can!"

Peace is attractive

Let us remember how attractive peace and love can be to someone who is looking for a church home. Harmony in the house of God is like a cool drink to a dry, thirsty soul who has just moved into our community. After the rigors of changing locations, schools and housing, families are anxious to join a fellowship that will help them feel settled in their new surroundings. A peaceful, growing church meets that very need. In a stressful world, full of confusion and contention, these words of our Lord bring comfort and security:

Peace I leave with you; my peace I give you. I do not give to you as the world gives. Do not let your hearts be troubled and do not be afraid. (John 14:27)

The churches that will demonstrate this message of peace and hope possess the potential for unprecedented growth. The congregation in conflict will never know the joy and fulfillment of that prospect.

Our Position in Discipleship

The term "discipleship" was finally laid to rest at the end of the 1970s. The concept enjoyed intense notoriety for several years. Parachurch organizations seemed to be scrambling to work this term into their logos and stationary designs. Churches were busy building "discipleship ministries" for the various age groups. Discipleship was the darling word of evangelicals for the better part of a decade.

As is often the case, a word overused may eventually become overlooked. Once popular terminology becomes trite and ultimately ignored. An adult using the terms "cool" or "heavy" around young people today would most likely evoke a blank stare. There was a time when everything, including hot pizza, was "cool." All pretty girls—even the thin ones—were "heavy, man." But these expressions are irrelevant now.

Though we have beaten the word "discipleship" to death, the concept should always be valid and vital in the body of Christ. It receives too much attention in Scripture to be overlooked by those who love God's Word. Discipleship has to do with the critical elements of identity, team and maturity. We make a monumental error in neglecting this principle.

Perhaps the privatization of North American society has contributed to this decline in an emphasis on biblical discipleship. People seem to be increasingly hesitant to share in the small group context today. Frightening visions of vulnerability and transparency haunt those who have been hurt previously in that setting. "I'll be fine just by myself, thank you."

Whereas Christians in the past were free to share personal struggles with each other, modern believers would make an appointment with a professional counselor or pastor. Our interaction in the body of Christ now is limited to brief, cute conversations about news, sports and weather as we sail through the church lobby. We gather in large groups on the Lord's day for Sunday school and worship services, and then rarely see one another through the week.

Too busy for discipleship

Today's believer is much too busy for discipleship. Most people seem to have one 60-hour-per-week job or two 30-hour-per-week jobs. Husbands and wives pass each other like so many ships in the night on their way to financial security or divorce—whichever comes first. Our teenagers are jumping in the car and riding off in four different directions hoping to save enough money for at least one month of college.

Our frantic pace today dictates that we put off "discipleship" until retirement. But by then, we probably wouldn't care.

Nevertheless, the number one reason for the deterioration in discipleship ministries just might be the intensification of conflict in the church. Our frequent fighting has made us reluctant to face one another for any length of time. We have learned to avoid contention by limiting our contact with each other.

Christ has some very important things to say to His church in this regard:

> A new command I give you: Love one another. As I have loved you, so you must love one another. By this all men will know that you are my disciples, if you love one another. (John 13:34–35)

John Calvin says of these two verses:

> As if Christ were saying, "While I am absent from you in body, testify by your mutual love, that you have not been taught by me in vain. Let this be your constant study, your chief meditation." . . .

> Since by this mark Christ distinguishes His own from strangers, those who discard love and adopt new and fabricated worship, labor in vain. (Calvin pp. 70–71)

"Fabricated worship." What a potent description of the services held in the combating church. "Labor in vain." What an appropriate portrayal of the futility inherent in trying to accomplish anything for the Lord when hatred permeates the house of God.

The corporate executive is known for his suit, tie and businesslike manner. The soldier is known for his uniform, discipline and dedication. The teacher is known for his or her wisdom and communication skill. The disciple of Jesus is to be known for his or her love.

Crowning characteristic

Agape love is the crowning characteristic of members in the body of Christ. We will have different hair styles and clothing. We may express our doctrines distinctively. Various kinds of music will be employed in our worship. But through it all, our Christian discipleship should be demonstrated through our love for each other.

Paul poses an interesting contrast to the Savior's command in his first letter to the Corinthians:

> You are still worldly. For since there is

jealousy and quarreling among you, are you not worldly? Are you not acting like mere men? (3:3)

The Apostle clearly indicates that the Corinthian believers were risking their very name for the sake of "jealousy and quarreling." They would be perceived as "mere men." In an ethical, behavioral sense, these people would be recognized on a purely human level. Their spiritual identity was hidden by the fervent rivalry with each other.

This is where many congregations begin to lose their character in the community. They put aside their association with true Christianity in order to pursue some disagreement within the church. They behave as if they do not even know Christ. The distinctives of discipleship have been lost amid internal strife.

Could this not be said of many of our board meetings and annual congregational gatherings? The "discipleship identity" has been compromised by those who choose to act as "mere men." Our actions and attitudes do not line up with our bold claim to be followers of Jesus Christ. We have placed more emphasis on being "right" than being "righteous."

The command of Christ in John 13:34–35 is another frightening reminder that our church conflict cannot be kept secret from the unchurched in the community. "By this all men will know that you are my disciples, if you love one another." If we do not love each other, the world will know something else—that we are hypocrites who give lip service to a Christian faith we do not live.

A sarcastic, skeptical world is waiting for the true church to resolve its own battles before it is willing to hear the gospel. Society has heard so much bad news about us that they are hesitant to listen to our good news. The congregation in conflict will lose its position in discipleship.

Our Power
in Evangelism

After several years with paper routes, my first real job as a teenager was in a grocery store—Geyer's Super Dollar Market. One of the cashiers in that supermarket was particularly annoying to me. It was passed off as a "personality clash." I said unkind things to this lady and talked behind her back.

During a spiritual awakening in my home church, God spoke clearly to me about my need to get things right with the cashier. I began to see the futility of trying to share Christ with other employees while gossiping about that woman at the cash register. I had been rendered ineffective in my witness by my bad attitudes and actions.

The confession was difficult in that I was asking forgiveness from those who did not know Christ or understand the need for repentance. But I not only cleared my conscience with the cashier. I also asked the other employees to forgive me for my poor example. Two years later, that lady was converted.

> Be ready at any time to give a quiet and reverent answer to any man who wants a reason for the hope that you have within you. Make sure that your conscience is perfectly clear, so that if men should speak slanderously of you as rogues, they may come to feel ashamed of themselves for libeling your good Christian behavior. (1 Peter 3:15–16, Phillips Translation)

The connection between a clear witness and a clean conscience is more than obvious. We simply cannot reach an individual for Christ if that person is harboring ill feelings toward us for some past offense. And our own bitterness for someone would most likely douse any desire to share the gospel with him.

This same principle applies on a larger scale in the church. It is improbable, if not impossible, for the congregation experiencing internal conflict to simultaneously reach out to evangelize its community. The war *within* the church will leave the parishioners powerless *outside* the church.

Devilish diversion
Battles in the body of Christ become a devilish diversion—a distraction. One pastor

said to me, "It has been a long time since our church has been able to look outwardly at the needs of lost people—we have been consumed inwardly by our strife and confusion. Satan has used this to get us away from what really matters, namely winning people to Christ."

It is indeed difficult to get people involved in "Evangelism Explosion" when the church itself is exploding with conflict. "Friendship Evangelism" tends to lose its appeal when God's people cannot be friends with each other. The Four Spiritual Laws become meaningless when Christians break the single most important law of God, "that we love one another."

From soul-centered to self-centered

This is doubtless the reason why many churches today have put aside every evangelistic strategy. These congregations have made a shift from being soul-centered to self-centered. They have lost their drive and desire for fulfilling the great commission.

In effect, these groups are just "putting in time" on Sundays and Wednesdays. This church goes through the motions of evangelical Christianity, but the reality is missing. Long board meetings ("bored" meetings) are filled with all the cute little details of day-to-day operations and the debate du jour. But no one mentions lost people headed for a Christless eternity. There are more important things on the agenda.

Is this not the most disturbing, devastating result of church conflict? Certainly it is pitiful to see a congregation lose its purpose for existence. It is tragic to see young people who feel Christianity is no longer plausible. To see a congregation's potential for growth frittered away by infighting is mournful. The misplacement of the discipleship identity is pathetic. But for a church to lose its power in evangelism . . . that is damnable!

Think of it! There are people lost in hell forever because of churches whose members spent their time and energy shouting at each other instead of sharing the gospel. Hearts that may have once been strangely warmed are turned cold and indifferent because of a feuding flock of God's people. Souls that were softened by the need for deliverance from sin become hardened and skeptical when exposed to explosive behavior in the church.

It is sad, but safe to say that some communities have no true gospel witness even though they may have several fundamental, evangelical churches. The unconverted have watched the "First" church split into a second and third congregation. They are familiar with the sordid and surprising details of each devastating split.

Maybe some of you reading these pages pride yourselves on being a troublemaker in your church. You enjoy the attention and power that conflict has bestowed upon you. Let me lovingly issue this stern warning: the blood of lost souls may be on your hands.

We are accountable

God's Word holds each of us accountable to present the way of salvation to "Jerusalem, Judea, Samaria, and the uttermost parts of the earth" (Acts 1:8b, KJV). When we hinder that process by our stubborn insistence to maintain an atmosphere of chaos, judgment will most certainly come upon us. "And if it begins with us, what will the outcome be for those who do not obey the gospel of God" (1 Peter 4:17b)?

In countless interviews with pastors, one striking comment was made on several occasions. Ministers told me of certain unruly parishioners who were standing in the way of evangelistic endeavor by their aggressive altercations. They prayed that the Lord would in some way remove them. Miraculously, some of them were transferred to another state, others contracted strange illnesses and a few even died.

There are scriptural precedents for the judgment of God on those who would hinder the spread of the gospel. In Acts 13:6–12 we find a shocking example. Elymas the sorcerer stood in opposition to Barnabas and Paul, trying "to turn Sergius Paulus from the faith." Paul moves quickly to condemn this obstructive, demonic force:

> You are a child of the devil and an enemy
> of everything that is right! You are full of
> all kinds of deceit and trickery. Will you
> never stop perverting the right ways of the
> Lord? (verse 10)

When this hindrance had been cleared away,
Sergius Paulus could readily accept the gospel.
"When the proconsul saw what had happened,
he believed, for he was amazed at the teaching
about the Lord" (verse 12).

This is a potent demonstration of God's attitude toward those who would impede the
propagation of His good news. Our Lord does
not look lightly upon that man, woman or
church that becomes a barrier to evangelization. It is perhaps the most serious offense that
could be imagined. Jesus said:

> Whoever welcomes a little child like this in
> my name welcomes me. But if anyone
> causes one of these little ones who believe
> in me to sin, it would be better for him to
> have a large millstone hung around his
> neck and to be drowned in the depths of
> the sea. (Matthew 18:5–6)

To "cause one of these little ones . . . to sin"
literally means to provide an occasion for them
to break God's law. One thinks of young Christians who are forced into the conflicts of a
strife-filled congregation. This is exactly what

Christ was condemning in the strongest possible language.

Do you see the blatant wickedness of church conflict in the light of lost men and women where you live? When a congregation loses its power in evangelism, it has lost everything. Our persistent warfare will certainly bring upon us that infamous name of "Ichabod"—the glory has departed.

Radical steps

I am familiar with congregations that began to see the grave implications of their rioting. Radical steps were taken to restore the relationship of the church to the community. Full page ads were taken out in local newspapers asking the entire town to forgive the congregation for its poor testimony. The personal principle from First Peter 3:15–16 was applied on a corporate level.

> But in your hearts set apart Christ as Lord. Always be prepared to give an answer to everyone who asks you to give the reason for the hope that you have. But do this with gentleness and respect, keeping a clear conscience, so that those who speak maliciously against your good behavior in Christ may be ashamed of their slander.

In each case, revival blessing flowed from this remarkable public repentance. Credibility was slowly regained as the church exemplified true Christianity. Parishioners sensed a new power in their personal witness for the Lord and souls were added to the kingdom through their efforts.

Vance Havner said, "It is often suggested that we should never expose sin in the professing church because it advertises the faults of believers to the world. Well, we are not telling the world anything it did not already know!" (Havner p. 54)

Church conflict has serious consequences. We jeopardize our purpose for existence, our position in discipleship, our plausibility among young people and our potential for growth. But the most sobering reality of all is our loss of power in evangelism.

PART III

RESOLVING CHURCH CONFLICT

Having looked at both reasons and results of church conflict, we can now take a more positive look at the issue of resolution. We have genuine cause for hope in the midst of our stormy struggles. God has provided clear and simple principles that will restore any congregation, making it fruitful and pleasing in His sight. As you read the closing chapters, apply these biblical concepts to your own local church struggles. Victory is on the way!

A Deeper Life
for Shallow Churches

Peeople are often surprised to find out that some of Hollywood's best and brightest stars are actually quite shy and insecure off stage. Their acting persona may be that of the macho man or woman who is in total control, but their private lives reveal just how vulnerable they can be. There is a sense in which these people lead two separate lives.

Athletes who may be graceful and incredibly accurate in their sport's discipline may have insurmountable personal problems just like the "average Joe." We now know that some of the world's finest athletes have had difficulties with drugs, alcohol and keeping a marriage intact. One personality shows up at the field, court or track. Another waits to take control after the game is over. *Dr. Jekyll and Mr. Hyde* comes to mind.

The Christian community is quick to point

out the double life that many people in the world seem to lead. However, the church today is plagued with its own evangelical version of a split personality. There is often a distinct dichotomy between our behavior on Sunday and our actions Monday through Saturday. This has contributed enormously to the high level of conflict in congregations.

For example, many church leaders approach the monthly board meeting with an attitude that says, "Well, we can put aside all 'spirituality' for the next few hours—it's time to get down to business!" Given that mentality, it should not surprise us to see so much bickering and confusion. We left our spiritual behavior at the boardroom door, so anything goes.

The choir assembles for its weekly practice. Rather than focusing on the great honor of ministry by singing for the Lord, many become embroiled in meaningless debates. Heated arguments arise concerning song selection, musical style or the imperfections of the director. Once again the perspective has been perverted. It is time for choir practice—so just forget about love, worship and other "spiritual" matters. Dr. Joyful Jekyll becomes Mr. Horrible Hyde.

The annual congregational meeting often becomes an illustration of this dual personality dilemma. Someone who appears calm and peaceful in a Sunday worship service may suddenly rise to state his or her case with carnal intonations. Small, seemingly insignificant items of business are blown out of proportion as people lay aside their Christian charity in order to stand their ground and demand their rights.

Danger of secularizing the sacred

Dr. A.W. Tozer pointed out the danger of secularizing the sacred:

> By accepting the world's values, thinking its thoughts and adopting its ways we have dimmed the glory that shines overhead. We have not been able to bring earth to the judgment of heaven so we have brought heaven to the judgment of the earth. Pity us, Lord, for we know not what we do! (Tozer p. 56)

Nicholas Herman, otherwise known as "Brother Lawrence," put things into their proper perspective:

> The time of business does not with me differ from the time of prayer, and in the noise and clatter of my kitchen, while at the same time several persons are at the same time calling for different things, I possess God in as great tranquility as if I were upon my knees at the blessed sacrament. (Herman p. 8)

How quickly things in our churches would change if we incorporated Romans 6:6–14 into our daily attitudes and actions:

> For we know that our old self was crucified with him so that the body of sin might be done away with, that we should no longer be slaves to sin . . . count your- selves dead to sin but alive to God in Christ Jesus. . . . Sin shall not be your master, because you are not under law but under grace.

Roy Hession, in *The Calvary Road*, says:

> The Lord Jesus cannot live in us fully and reveal Himself through us until the proud self within us is broken. This simply means that the hard unyielding self, which justifies itself, wants its own way, stands up for its rights, and seeks its own glory, at last bows its head to God's will, admits its wrong, gives up its own way to Jesus, surrenders its rights and discards its own glory—that the Lord Jesus might have all and be all. In other words, it is dying to self and self-attitudes. (Hession p. 22)

This is the kind of practical holiness that will lead to conflict resolution. As a congregation, starting with its leadership, embraces this posi- tion in Christ, our point of reference radically shifts from "me" and "my agenda" to "Christ" and "His agenda." There will no longer be a need for bruised and battered saints to sing, "I did it my way!"

Power-hungry parishioners would realize that the carnal drive for control is a manifestation of the old nature—that "old self" that died along with Christ on Mount Calvary. We are no longer amenable to an ego-centered life-style.

> When we were controlled by the sinful nature, the sinful passions aroused by the law were at work in our bodies, so that we bore fruit for death. But now, by dying to what once bound us, we have been released from the law so that we serve in the new way of the Spirit, and not in the old way of the written code. (Romans 7:5–6)

Pastors need not feel under pressure to make sure of votes before a board meeting in this "new way of the Spirit." They can rest in the Lord rather than in human persuasion and manipulation. The issue is no longer, "Do I have enough leaders on my side for this vote?" What really matters is that the minister himself is on God's side.

Brokenness is lacking
It is this kind of brokenness before the Lord

and one another that is so sadly lacking in our relationships with fellow believers. We have become mesmerized by the power politics of a society that insists on promoting self at any cost. We have been taught to push our idea and jockey for the best position. We are reminded to "never take 'no' for an answer," and to hold our head high. In the words of Shirley MacLaine in *Going Within*, "The only source is ourselves." (p. 29)

Jesus Christ emphatically disagrees. One of the primary prerequisites for following Jesus is that one must "deny himself and take up his cross daily and follow" Him (Luke 9:23). Dr. Tozer points out that to "deny" oneself basically means to "forget" about oneself. The essence of discipleship is to place the agenda of Christ and others before our own. And odd as it may seem, it is only in such self denial that we discover genuine self fulfillment. "Whoever loses his life for me will save it" (Luke 9:24).

An illustration

To illustrate, let's say that the worship leader and the choir director are bickering over what should be sung next Sunday. Both have good, sound reasons for selecting their numbers. Both could present a convincing argument. But one of them has to deny him or herself for the sake of peace and harmony. Someone must give up their own way in Christlike selflessness.

This self-denying, Christ-exalting mentality

would have an immediate impact on daily deliberations and decisions of the church. New attitudes would be prevalent among nursery workers. Building committee meetings would never be the same again once God's people were intent on considering others better than themselves (Philippians 2:3). Different attitudes would become immediately apparent among soloists and singing groups.

If all this sounds somewhat idyllic, it is only because, as I once heard Leonard Ravenhill say, "The church is so subnormal that God's normal looks abnormal!" Watchman Nee calls this "the normal Christian life." In Ephesians 5:18 Paul commanded every believer to "be being filled with the Spirit." The deeper life, characterized by death to self and life in the Spirit, should indeed be the standard for all true believers.

Time to confront

We have too many dead churches full of believers who are alive to the flesh. Our need is for congregations that are alive and full of Christians who are dead to the flesh! Perhaps it is time to lovingly confront some self-serving, flesh-fulfilling leaders in the church—this may include pastors, board members, musicians, Sunday school personnel and others. Only the practice of the deeper life will rescue us from the mediocrity of superficial lives and shallow churches.

Perhaps a pastor should poll his leaders or

congregation at large. Ask the questions: "What are some areas where we need to apply 'death to self' and 'fullness of the Spirit'? In what areas of church life have we allowed the flesh to get the upperhand? Are you experiencing victory over the old nature in your personal life?"

Dr. A.B. Simpson asks:

> How shall we win the victory over self? . . . We must definitely and thoroughly enter into the meaning of that mighty word, "Ye are not your own." We must surrender ourselves so utterly that we can never own ourselves again. We must hand over self and all its rights in an eternal covenant, and give God the absolute right to own us, control us, and possess us forever. And we must abide in this attitude, and never recall that irrevocable surrender. (Simpson p. 28)

Maybe someone reading these pages needs to take a fresh journey to Calvary. What is required is a renewed gaze upon the Savior who died that we might live in victory over carnal passions that war within the soul. Visualize the crucified and risen Christ in His glorious triumph over self, death and hell. But most importantly, remember that it was for you—for your daily joy and success as a believer. His

victory means that we can enjoy right relationships with God and one another.

Confess your self-centeredness for the tragic
sin that it is. Believe God for the cleansing
wave of the blood of Christ. Then ask the Lord
to fill you anew and afresh with the precious
Holy Spirit. Trust Him to do exactly as you request regardless of your emotional state.

As the Lord is faithful to point out people
who have been offended through your carnal
behavior, make the necessary restitution. This
is not the easy way, but it is the best way. It is
useless to sit back hoping that people will
notice the change in our hearts when we are
unwilling to humble ourselves. It is relatively
easy to express our brokenness before God, but
our biggest test will come with the people in
the pews.

When Christians begin to see how the old nature has ruined relationships and decimated
the church, hearts will once again seek the Lord
in all His fullness. We will pray in the words of
Dr. Simpson:

> O Jesus, come and dwell in me,
> Walk in my steps each day,
> Live in my life, love in my love,
> And speak in all I say;
> Think in my thoughts, let all my acts
> Thy very actions be,
> So shall it be no longer I,
> But Christ that lives in me. (Simpson p. 31)

CHAPTER

19

Back to the Bible

The Allen family takes Monopoly very seriously. No single game has brought about more laughter, tears, conflict and confusion in our home. Many matches have ended with participants proclaiming that they would absolutely, positively never play Monopoly again. Their decision was final and irrevocable. Nothing could or would ever change their mind.

But 24 hours later, we would unfold that game board, shuffle the "Chance" and "Community Chest" cards, distribute the money, roll the dice and go on another wild ride into the danger zone. There was an irresistible urge to find out if today things just might go your way. Hotels would be erected on Boardwalk and Park Place, as well as the "greens" and "reds." Everyone would land on your loaded properties and unload their money into your account. Parker Brothers had indeed created a monster.

Certain phrases became famous during our

world championship Monopoly matches. When someone owed a large sum of money, and offered property for the payoff, they would often hear in a soft whisper, "cold cash." The deal-making rhetoric was incredible. "This is a once-in-a-lifetime offer!" "You will never see another trade like this again!" "It appears that you are going to lose, and I just want to help."

Through the years, I developed a philosophy of winning that even turned defeats into victories. The strategy was simple: protest every little minor infraction so as to keep the competition on edge. By the end of the game, no matter who actually "won," the real "winner" was the one who gained the upperhand psychologically. The object was to make sure that the victor did not enjoy his or her triumph.

The truth of the matter is that we asked for all the confusion and conflict. I am the eighth of 10 children. My older brothers and sisters told me that many years ago they decided to throw away the Monopoly rulebook. (I would have never known that any rules existed if it were not for this frank confession by family members.) "Every man did what was right in his own eyes."

When friends and neighbors attempted to join in the fray, they were amazed at how thoroughly we had dispensed with the Parker Brother's regulations. But being the eighth child, I never knew any other way to play

Monopoly. Something about the lack of absolutes seemed to make it all more interesting. And it certainly made it more combative.

We've discarded the rulebook

It occurs to me that congregations are in conflict today because the church, too, has discarded the rulebook. We have neglected clear teachings in God's Word. This has resulted in an abundance of unnecessary revelry. Resolution will reveal itself only as we get back to the Bible.

In a chapter from *Man: The Dwelling Place of God* entitled, "The Importance of Sound Doctrine," A.W. Tozer says:

> Each generation of Christians must look to its beliefs. While truth itself is unchanging, the minds of men are porous vessels out of which error may seep to dilute the truth they contain. The human heart is heretical by nature and runs to error as naturally as a garden to weeds. All a man, a church or a denomination needs to guarantee deterioration of doctrine is to take everything for granted and do nothing. (p. 162)

Consider earlier chapters in Part I—the reasons for church conflict. Does Scripture have anything at all to say about the nature of true worship? Would not a diligent Bible study of this subject help us solve some of our differences regarding styles of worship? We might be surprised with the findings of believers who would approach the subject with an open mind and heart.

The Word of God addresses the issue of music and its ministry in the church. We are clearly instructed to make sure that our music draws attention primarily to the Master rather than the musicians. Our songs and hymns are to be "spirit"-related rather than "flesh"-related. Music that "feels right" may not always be good for us. God is honored by lyrics and lifestyles that lift up the name of Jesus Christ. Should we not dig into Scripture for a biblical view of music instead of immediately judging the motives of others who think differently?

Congregations squabble over the role of women in the church. But when will we commission a thorough investigation of the Bible on this issue? This is not the responsibility of the district office or the denominational leaders—each fellowship is accountable to discover God's will in this matter.

Scripture has a few things to say about the role of the pastor in his preaching ministry. Getting back to the Bible is our only hope for finding a balance in this day of great expectations. Persecution in the pulpit will continue as long as we ignore the Word of God.

The Bible gives unclouded instruction on how to handle money problems and doctrinal debates. We are informed on the proper reaction to gossip and unfair discipline. Christ did not leave us guessing about how power and authority are to be exercised in the church. We are told of God's desire for congregations to grow both quantitatively and qualitatively in His Word. And First Corinthians 12 to 14 provides a balanced picture that will not lead us to either charismania or charisphobia.

We refuse to act on Scripture

So many times congregations simply refuse to act on Scripture, even if it will correct a problem. Consider this example.

As a pastor, I ran into a situation where biblical principles were being violated in the marriage of a governing board member. It was a situation, unfortunately, that most churches would not deal with since it didn't seem like a big deal. His wife was clearly in charge and he was not taking steps to reorder the home according to Ephesians 5:22–25.

After discussing it with the elders, I asked the couple to meet with me. I simply reiterated the scriptural teachings with which they were already familiar. I told the husband that he could not continue in his leadership role in the church until he assumed his biblical role of leadership at home. "If anyone does not know how to manage his own family, how can he take care of God's church" (1 Timothy 3:5)?

The Lord enabled both the husband and the wife to see the serious need in their marriage.

He stepped quietly aside from his position on the board. One year later, substantial progress had been made. God's Word had made a difference in that marriage. I fully endorsed his nomination to the governing board at the next election and he was welcomed back with love and respect.

Remember: "All Scripture is God-breathed and is useful for teaching, rebuking, correcting and training in righteousness, so that the people of God may be thoroughly equipped for every good work" (2 Timothy 3:16–17). But, the Word of God must be allowed to do the teaching, the rebuking, the correcting and the training in righteousness. It's all in the Book. Our Lord left nothing out that we would need to live a holy, productive life personally and corporately.

Some would argue, appropriately so, that the Bible is silent on several of the "finer details." This cannot be contested. But the overriding principles of the Word have to do with our reaction to those who disagree with us. Many issues call upon us to simply "agree to disagree agreeably." Such matters will not be settled to everyone's satisfaction in this life, only when we get to heaven.

No dedication to the Word

We are no longer dedicated to the Holy Word of God as our source of authority, information and inspiration. This has produced a sort of "evangelical humanism." Many believers have adopted an attitude that says, "It's my opinion versus your opinion, and there are no absolutes." That works well in the secular classroom. Those teachers and students refuse to acknowledge the Bible as the final authority on anything. Christians, however, should know better.

We must replace our conflicts with the conquest of God's truth as revealed in Scripture. We should pour our energy and intellectual gifts into the discovery of those principles that will bring solutions to our fiery debates. When confronted with dilemmas that have no black and white answers, we can appeal to those passages that call us to a Christlike humility and servant spirit.

Both Monopoly and the ministry can be miserable when we throw out the rulebook. Losses sustained in the playing of a board game will be silly and short term. But the stakes are much higher when the church discards its only rulebook, God's Word. Getting back to the Bible means getting back to harmony, growth and outreach. This we must do if our conflicts are to be resolved.

The Discipline of the Saints

As I write this chapter, I am entering my 10th year as a father. Two darling daughters, Andrea and Mandi, have taught my wife and me many valuable lessons. Most parents begin with the notion that they will do all the teaching. But it doesn't take long to realize that mom and dad must also be students.

One of the most surprising lessons we have learned from our girls is that they understand their need for a balance of love and discipline. We easily assumed that they were well aware of the importance of being loved. Human nature craves affection and attention. However, our daughters also recognize the necessity for firm, consistent discipline.

This is not to imply that punishment is always received with enthusiasm and joy around our house! But there is a recognition of the fact that certain lines must not be crossed, and when they are, godly parents must swiftly intervene to rescue children from their own folly.

This is often painful in the present, but our family recognizes that it could only get worse in the future if we fail to deal with the current disobedience.

The results of timid or nonexistent leadership in the home are evident for all to see today. Young people are running wild in the streets with no sense of right or wrong. Women are raped, stores are robbed and the authorities are ridiculed. We have spared the rod, spoiled the child, and spun out of control.

Parallels can unfortunately be drawn to the church. Too many pastors and parishioners are sauntering through our sanctuaries unchecked and unaccountable to anyone for anything. Rebellious souls are running wild through our ranks, and no one is lifting a finger to stop them.

We need biblical discipline

So many congregations could have been spared years of anguish and infighting if we were willing to practice biblical church discipline. If just once someone could have lovingly confronted that renegade board member with his passion for power and his delight in dissention, a dead congregation might be alive today.

I think of that man referred to in chapter 9 who said to the new pastor, "I've gotten rid of six pastors before you, and I can get rid of you, too!" Others in the church knew of this man's devious schemes over a period of 30 years. But he was never challenged to deal with his blatant, sinful insubordination. That church was small, is small, and will be small until he repents, relocates or dies.

In a church that I pastored, there was one particular woman who just thrived on gossip. (Men have that problem, too, but in this case it was a woman.) She loved to spread rumors and hear them. To send a message, you could telephone, telegraph or tell her. She was constantly stirring up the embers of conflict.

Periodically, I had to bring her into my office and confront her with the latest innuendo she had been sharing. One time it became obvious that the gossip had infected a large number in the congregation so I asked her to publicly ask forgiveness for the hurtful heresay she had been propagating.

Pastors need to be disciplined, too

Countless congregations might be thriving today if their pastor had been disciplined years ago. But he moves from church to church, across state and district lines, repeating the same patterns of corruption and conflict. The results of his ministry are as predictable as the sunrise. One could almost name the year and the month that he will be forced to move on to the next parish (perish?).

I have talked with many bishops and super-intendents about this pressing problem. Many are reluctant to tackle the tough issues surrounding pastoral discipline. Some of the ministers who need spiritual correction are in large, influential churches. Repercussions could spread for many miles. The excuses are numerous and impressive, but thoroughly unscriptural.

"Brothers, if someone is caught in a sin, you who are spiritual should restore him gently. But watch yourself, or you also may be tempted" (Galatians 6:1).

"Restore" here means to reinstate the individual to a proper spiritual condition or to a right mind. This is the very essence of church discipline. It is to be carried out in the context of genuine humility with a goal of renewing the fallen brother or sister to correct thinking and behavior.

Four-stage approach

In Matthew 18:15–17, Christ outlines a four-stage approach to discipline that will lead to either restoration or rejection. It starts with the offended party lovingly confronting the offender with his or her sin. If the transgressor refuses to acknowledge the offense, it is to be taken to the small group setting: "take one or two others along." Should this fail to induce repentance, the church is to be notified, whereupon any lack of remorse should lead to expulsion from the fellowship.

The goal of church discipline is still intact: "If

he listens to you, you have won your brother over." It's all about winning our brother over, restoring broken relationships, renewing spiritual life and effectiveness.

Talk to one another

Notice the word "listens" ("If he listens to you"). We often miss this important principle. We are to talk to one another about problems in the church, and the sooner the better. If we can deal with dilemmas at their inception, we are much more apt to succeed in our damage control.

Much of our conversation in churches these days is "about" or "behind" or "around" someone. We fail to talk directly "to" the person involved. In churches where I pastored, I told my leadership to come to me first when they heard criticism about something I had said or done. And I promised to go directly to them, too, in the reverse situation.

My father passed along a little gem that applies here: "Keep short accounts." Don't let walls build up so that you can't see over them. Deal with difficulties the moment they arise. If you need to ask forgiveness, do it now. If something or someone must be lovingly confronted, do it now. Refuse to let little things become monstrous because of fear or neglect.

Fear of negative reaction

We fear negative reaction to spiritual correction to such an extreme that we miss the positive result. People who were thinking and acting in an unscriptural manner can be turned around through loving discipline. Those who misused power can become a miracle of God's power to transform.

This chapter ties in rather neatly with the previous chapter on getting back to the Bible. As we have gotten away from our dependence on Scripture, we have neglected the necessity to chastise our fallen brothers and sisters. God's Word instructs us plainly along these lines, and church conflict will not be resolved until we once again practice the discipline of the saints.

As indicated in chapter seven, the mishandling of spiritual correction in the body of Christ can have tragic consequences. This is no doubt why some are a bit "gun shy" about dealing with sin in the church. Nevertheless, the decision to discipline the saints should not be based on past successes or failures. We can learn from our mistakes without disregarding this important ministry.

What needs to be said most here is that we are all struggling with a very basic desire: self-preservation. Everyone of us wants to be loved. We have a natural resistance to controversy. District leaders want to be popular with their pastors and churches. Personnel in denominational headquarters want to have a good relationship with the superintendents and pastors. Ministers want to be loved by their congregations. People want to be fondly regarded by the minister and his family.

When church discipline becomes necessary, all of those good feelings we want to generate are jeopardized. Enormous risk is involved, even in a legal sense today, when steps must be taken to restore a fallen brother or sister. The problem is compounded when the offending person refuses to repent or even recognize the fact that he or she was wrong.

Costly not to discipline

In the short term, it may seem very costly and dangerous to practice biblical discipline. Just the opposite is true. The price and the peril increase dramatically when we ignore this obligation. Evidence abounds to demonstrate the devastation in churches where they would not follow through with this difficult, unenviable task.

"But if I attempt to deal with that person in my church, some families will certainly leave. This guy is very popular, and I'm afraid that the people will take sides." We must accept the fact that we may lose some people for the sake of spiritual housecleaning. Not everyone will agree with our methods though they may be strictly by the Book.

God will protect us from making major blunders in this area if our motivation remains pure. As we seek to restore rather than ridicule the erring child of the kingdom, our churches will be strengthened and Christ will be honored.

We make a mistake when we assume that church discipline is limited only to "serious" cases involving adultery, embezzlement or heresy. We must care enough to confront brothers and sisters who are spreading gossip. Someone must get that self-centered individual aside and point him or her to Calvary. It is paramount that we deal immediately with the bitterness that flows so freely from some people.

Indeed, the greatest impact of scriptural discipline will be felt in the arena of church conflict. As pastors and parishioners are challenged to deal with bad attitudes, gossip, divisiveness, pride, power struggles and a host of other contentious sins, love and unity can be restored in the fellowship.

In the late 60s, my dad was not always the most popular man around the house. The miniskirt fad was in full swing, and my sisters were not allowed to be in style. Some good fights took place. Those were days of high drama around the house, and I would be lying to say I didn't enjoy it. I was, after all, a boy, a brother, and a brat.

But my father established high standards and kept them. The interesting footnote is that some of his daughters wrote him after they were married to say, "Dad, thanks for holding the line." Bill Allen was willing to trade off his popularity in the short term for lifelong respect. He had the sneaking suspicion that someday mature daughters would understand why Dad didn't want his girls enticing young men in a sensual manner. Eventually they would see that he had their best interests at heart.

Church discipline can have this same happy ending. If we are willing to do what is necessary instead of what is comfortable, we, too, can enjoy the long-term love and respect of those around us. Settling for the pseudo-peace of the present will only pave the way for heartache in the future. God's way is not always the easiest, but it is certainly the best.

> My son, do not make light of the
>   Lord's discipline,
> and do not lose heart when he
>   rebukes you,
> because the Lord disciplines those he
>   loves,
> and he punishes everyone he accepts
>   as a son. (Hebrews 12:5-6)

EPILOGUE

The Revival We Need

Shirley MacLaine says of evangelicalism, "The various churches were not fulfilling our needs. Besides that, their leadership, in part, was corrupt. . . . We were left with no recourse but ourselves." (MacLaine p. 43)

Indeed, "The greatest tragedy in our world today is a sick church in a dying world," says Leonard Ravenhill. (p. 53) Fortunately for us, "the sickness is not unto death." There is hope for the patient because God is the doctor.

There is little argument about our great need for a heaven-sent, Holy Spirit revival among evangelical Christians. But few seem able or willing to identify the "kind" of revival that is required to restore the effectiveness of the church's ministry in an increasingly complex world.

John Nasbitt, in *Megatrends 2000*, speaks of a renewed interest in "religion" at the close of the 20th century. But he makes a point, no doubt valid, that the shift will be more in the

171

direction of the New Age movement because of its openness to a broad spectrum of religious thought. (Nasbitt pp. 270–297)

This is not the revival we need. But it may be the one we will get if the true church does not rise above its petty conflicts to demonstrate the relevance of Christ in the life of 21st-century mankind. We are distancing ourselves from society by our internal warfare, and false cults are beginning to reap our harvest.

Two revivals needed

First, we need a REVIVAL OF REPEN-TANCE. "There is too much spreading cold cream on cancers and dusting off sin with a powder puff," said the late Vance Havner. (p. 54) The church must rediscover the importance of genuine repentance—a godly sorrow for sin, a change of mind and a change of action.

Individuals involved in church conflict must repent. We should feel sorrow for the way we have abused the wonderful name of Christ for the sake of having our own way. We need to change our mind about attitudes that have long dominated our thinking. We must ask God to give us power to change our behavior.

During one of my earliest revival meetings as a young evangelist, I saw the Lord turn a church in Pontiac, Michigan completely around in 48 hours. In the opening service on a Friday night, the pianist stopped playing in the middle of the invitation hymn. She was weeping profusely and eventually left the piano bench to go to the altar. Others quickly joined her. Bitter feuds that had been seething for years were resolved through sincere repentance in a matter of minutes. Pastor/people conflicts melted away in the intense heat of confession and restitution. I learned there and then the vital connection between repentance and the resolution of strife in a congregation.

Personalize this for a moment: are YOU willing to repent of any sin that God would mercifully reveal in order to see an end to the distressing discord? Will YOU agree with God concerning anything He might want to show YOU?

Second, we need a REVIVAL OF RELEVANCE. The evangelical church must once again demonstrate the fact that it has something significant to say to modern man. We can recover from our integrity crisis only by practicing what we preach.

The man on the street glances skeptically at the "born-again Christian" as if to say, "Why should I follow Christ? Can 2,000-year-old teachings relate to me and my life here and now?" Our mission is to be able to answer these inquiries in an understandable, winsome way.

Our world is filled with conflict. Families are fighting and torn apart. People are resigning from jobs because of stress and strife at the office. We have an incredible opportunity to display the relevance of Christianity by showing how Christ enables us to resolve our disputes.

"Conflict Management" is a popular phrase in business today because corporations know that bottom-line productivity is directly related to peace in the workplace. Should not the church be leading the way in this matter?

God's Word and the Christian faith are more than relevant to the needs of our world. We have a solemn responsibility to use an old message with new methods to win as many as possible before our Lord returns. Repentance and relevance . . . the revival we need.

Let me suggest that you put this book down, get on your knees, and say with the Psalmist, "Search me, O God." As we cooperate with the Spirit, the Lord will take care of the rest.

> Lord, I have heard of your fame;
>   I stand in awe of your deeds, O Lord.
> Renew them in our day,
>   in our time make them known;
>   in wrath remember mercy.
>   (Habakkuk 3:2)

Bibliography

Calvin, John. *The Gospel According to St. John.* Grand Rapids, MI: Eerdmans Publishing Company, 1959.

Grosvenor, Mary and Zerwick, Max. *A Grammatical Analysis of the Greek New Testament.* Rome: Biblical Institute Press, 1981.

Havner, Vance. *Road to Revival.* Old Tappan, NJ: Fleming H. Revell Company, 1950.

Hermon, Nicholas. *The Practice of the Presence of God.* Old Tappan, NJ: Fleming H. Revel Company, 1958.

Hession, Roy. *The Calvary Road.* Fort Washington, PA: Christian Literature Crusade, 1950.

Lutzer, Erwin. *Flames of Freedom.* Chicago: Moody Press, 1976.

MacLaine, Shirley. *Going Within.* New York: Bantam, 1989.

Naisbitt, John and Aburdene, Shirley. *Megatrends 2000*. New York: William Morrow and Company, Inc., 1990.

Ravenhill, Leonard. *America is Too Young To Die*. Minneapolis: Bethany Fellowship, Inc., 1979.

———. *Why Revival Tarries*. Minneapolis: Bethany Fellowship, Inc., 1974.

Shelley, Marshall. *Well Intentioned Dragons: Ministering to Problem People in the Church*. *Leadership Library*. Carol Stream, IL: Christianity Today, Inc., Word Inc., 1985.

Simpson, Albert B. *Victory Over Self*. Camp Hill, PA: Christian Publications, Inc.

Tozer, A.W. *Man: The Dwelling Place of God*. Camp Hill, PA: Christian Publications, Inc., 1966.

Verwer, George. *Come! Live! Die!* Wheaton, IL: Tyndale House Publishers, 1972.

Wilmoth, Eileen, ed. *365 Devotions*. Cincinnati, OH: The Standard Publishing Company, 1989.

For additional copies of
Congregations in Conflict
contact your local Christian bookstore
or call Christian Publications, toll-free,
1-800-233-4443.

God has uniquely prepared Tom Allen
for ministry in the areas of family, church
growth, church leadership, church conflict and
effective evangelism. If your church would
like to contact Tom about the possibility of
ministering, Christian Publications would be
happy to put you in touch with him.